A RUSTIC MORALIST

A RUSTIC MORALIST

BY

WILLIAM RALPH INGE

FORMERLY DEAN OF ST. PAUL'S

Author of *Lay Thoughts of a Dean,*
More Lay Thoughts of a Dean, etc.

G. P. Putnam's Sons

NEW YORK

Printed in Great Britain by
UNWIN BROTHERS LIMITED, LONDON AND WOKING

PREFACE

Ecce iterum Crispinus! Did not Dr. Inge take an affecting farewell of his public in 1934? Did he not almost promise, in his little book called *Vale*, not to waste any more ink and paper on his senile reflections? I did; I meant to keep my resolution; I have no excuse for breaking it. A too indulgent editor and a too indulgent publisher must bear and share the blame.

Have I anything fresh to say? Have I modified any of the opinions which I have so often inflicted upon long-suffering readers? I have at least not ceased to read and think about religion, philosophy, and public affairs.

I have long been thoroughly dissatisfied with the prevailing trend of modern philosophy. The spirit of modern thought is anti-intellectual. "It has become the fashion," says the able Indian thinker, Radhakrishnan, "to idealize impulse over reason, sentiment over thought, and to denounce all system-making." Or, as the American philosopher Perry puts it, "psychology, speaking for emotion and instinct, has reduced intellect to impotence over life; metaphors have subordinated it to the will. Bergson and his followers have charged it with falsehood, while with Pragmatists and Instrumentalists it has sunk so low that it is dressed in livery and sent to live in the servants' quarters." William

5

James, the champion of anti-intellectualism, declares that "Our faith beforehand in an uncertified result is the only thing that makes a result come true"—truth being merely a name for whatever *works*. "Truth is not an end of dialectics," says Dr. Schiller; it is merely "a preliminary means to other vital satisfactions." "It is a mark of great coarseness to wish to be right," says Le Roy, not to be outdone by his American and English friends; "it is a testimony of a great want of culture."

It would obviously be impossible in this short preface either to explain this strange revolt against realism or to give reasons for rejecting it. But it is all-pervading. Even science is reducing itself to mathematical formulas, with no necessary relation to reality; the astronomers coquet with Berkeleyan idealism, and forget that they began with very concrete "stars and atoms," which they treated as real objects.

In religion, as Urban says, modernism turns the absolutes of religion into the relatives of an evolutionary process; psychology reduces faith to a mere instinct in the service of life. In art also, absolutes have everywhere given place to relatives, truth to impressionism, the complete subjectivism of art reflecting itself in the denial of all standards of aesthetic value. (I have let myself go on this subject in two of these little essays.)

How does the idea of God fare with these modernist thinkers? If He exists at all, He is organic with the world, which is as necessary to Him as He is to it. He appears under strange names—Space-Time, a Nisus, the Divinal Imaginal, Duration, the Great Toiler, the President of the Cosmic Commonwealth (the Americans are very emphatic that democracy has no use for a non-elected king). A mathematician, it has been suggested, might pray to x^n.

None of these theories is reconcilable with Christianity, which is not hospitable to every philosophy, but has, as I am increasingly convinced, a philosophy of its own. This I find most lucidly expounded in the Roman Catholic Neo-Thomists, such as Gilson and Maritain in France, and especially Sheen, an American professor at Louvain. I neither know nor care what the venomous Roman Catholic journalists, who are always abusing me as an enemy of their Church, may make of this. There is no inconsistency whatever, and very little change in my views. When Gilson says at the beginning of his Gifford Lectures that "Christian philosophy is the spirit of Christianity penetrating the Greek tradition, working within it, drawing out of it a certain view of the world," that is what I have always maintained myself. These writers find the main source of modernist errors in the confusion of "reason" with the higher faculty of "intellect" or "intelligence." When William James boasts that he has killed "that beast, Intellect," he might have spared his excitement if he had taken the trouble to find out what *Nous* meant to the Greeks, and *Intellectus* to the Latins. I think there are signs of a return to what Catholics call "the perennial philosophy," even among non-Christians; but the wish may be father to the thought.

At the same time, I feel strongly that rationalism has its limits. There are some facts, such as the existence of the world, for which we can give no reason; we must just accept it. Nor are the mysteries connected with time and space soluble— even by putting a hyphen between them. The absolute values—Truth, Goodness, and Beauty— cannot be rationalized; they are ultimates. And since religion rests on belief in these values, as objective revelations of the mind of God, we are driven to poetry, symbol, and myth to make the invisible real to ourselves. This is how Plato used his myths, and no religion—no philosophy even—can dispense with them. From this follows the utter impossibility of imposing a stereotyped orthodoxy on all alike. This I have urged in my little allegory of the clergy as spectacle makers.

These, I think, are the directions in which my thoughts about religion and philosophy have chiefly run since my retirement. I am of course quite out of Church politics now, and I am not sure whether there are any Church politics. Reunion, in the sense of a corporate amalgamation of the Anglican communion with any other religious body, is out of the question. The overtures of Lord Halifax and

8

his friends to the uncompromising Roman Church were childish and humiliating, and the admission of other Protestant pastors to officiate at our altars would split the Church of England from top to bottom. Mutual recognition, however, is quite possible, except in the case of the Latin Church. Successful attempts have been made to obtain this recognition from the Rumanian Church, and it seems likely that the whole of the Eastern Orthodox Church may be brought to admit the validity of our Orders, as we have always admitted the validity of theirs. Mutual recognition at home is much more important, but as far as I can see it must be approached unofficially and illegally.

I have asked for permission to reprint my devotional address on "Prayer," read at the Conference of Modern Churchmen last summer, because it was grotesquely and rather maliciously misrepresented by several newspapers.

On home politics my views are unchanged. The Devil, according to Dr. Johnson, was the first Whig; perhaps the ex-Dean of St. Paul's is the last. That is to say, I am in favour of peace and retrenchment, and I regret the tendency on both sides to make politics simply what I have called an auction of the worldly goods of the minority. There is no help for it. Power is always abused, and politicians must live. It is too early to predict the ultimate consequences of the vast extension of "social services" on our national life. At present, the majority are certainly better off than they were before the war; but the effect of pushing up wages, by political pressure, above the economic level has been to increase the problem of unemployment, a complex phenomenon which cannot be attributed to any single cause. It is to be feared that many who are out of work can never be employed, because their labour is not worth the minimum wage which they would be allowed to accept. The system of doles has also stopped emigration, a subject with which I have dealt in this book. It seems to me that we are throwing away the opportunity of creating several new Britains overseas, an opportunity which we shall certainly never have again. I have argued that State action to subsidize colonization on a large scale would be thoroughly justified.

A hereditary landed aristocracy is theoretically as indefensible as a hereditary monarchy. But both have been integral parts of the social life of our nation for many centuries, and they are not a severe drain on the resources of a wealthy country. I am sorry to see the old country houses everywhere abandoned or destroyed, though I need hardly say that there are few positions which I myself would not choose in preference to that of a sporting squire.

The parrot-like babblings of our callow young intellectuals, who hypnotize themselves with catchwords like *proletarian*, *bourgeois*, *capitalism*, *wage-slavery*, *a dying social order*, have no relation to realities in this country or any other. Bernard Shaw was quite right when he said that Marx has never got hold of the British working man, and never will. Large scale organization no doubt has a future, though it is far more difficult than the advocates of "planned economy" realize; but in England at any rate it is almost certain to remain within the limits of the existing social order. We are in fact becoming a nation of small *rentiers*, a timidly conservative class. The prophets of academic socialism seem to have one feature in common—a complete ignorance of practical business.

When I think of the alarming unrest of the earlier decades of the nineteenth century, the aftermath of the war with Napoleon, and of the comparative contentment, quiet and prosperity which followed them, I am not at all sure that we may not be approaching a period of stable equilibrium, a pleasanter time to live in than that in which our lot is cast.

It is very difficult to find anything wise to say about foreign politics. The destruction of liberty over the greater part of Europe, and the establishment of new types of dictatorship in several countries, took us all by surprise. We had become so much accustomed to talk about the irresistible march of democracy that the ignominious collapse of our idol, after a very feeble resistance, upset all our most cherished beliefs. The devout hymns which Americans still intone to their fetish seem to us almost pathetic. But there are one or two prophecies which I shall be rash enough to make.

The opinion on the Continent is that we are approaching a new and terrible European war. Here again I will have the courage of my opinions and say that I do not believe it. The conditions are quite unlike those of 1914. Then all the great nations were rich; their credit stood high. Although the cost of the war far surpassed all expectations, they found it possible to finance it by borrowing. But most of the war-debts were repudiated, so that in future no one will look on war-loan as an investment. At the present time all the nations which might be suspected of desiring war, except Russia, are virtually bankrupt. We are often told that a nation can always pay its soldiers as it goes along. I do not believe it. I do not believe that either Germany or Italy could finance a great war. Germany is in such a plight financially that I have grave doubts whether the Hitler regime can last out the year; and Italy is not in a much better case. Italian militarism seems to be merely a perverted romanticism, like that which brought Napoleon to his ruin. A revival of the Mediterranean empire of ancient Rome is a fantastic dream. The conditions for its realization do not exist.

Nor could Germany attack Russia, which would by aided by France, with any chance of success. Russia, which is moving cautiously in the direction of an industrial and peasant republic, is more stable, both politically and financially, than Germany, where a declaration of war would release a huge volume of violent discontent against the existing regime. The German bayonets are not for use against France, still less against ourselves. The Germans are honestly afraid of the immense Russian army and of a Communist rising within their own borders.

The civil war in Spain may be the precursor of similar international struggles elsewhere. Nationalism, which has lately seemed to make a stronger appeal to modern Europeans than any other call, whether religious or social, may in the long run prove to be less potent than other idealisms, which make little of old-fashioned patriotism. We may have a series of revolts, subsidized and assisted by foreign governments, and fought out amid such horrors as Europe has not seen since the so-called Wars of Religion. This, in my opinion, is a greater danger than the menace of a renewal of the Great War. Fanaticism is the most cruel spirit in the world; fear comes next to it.

The miscellaneous articles in this collection must be left to justify their resurrection if they can. The writing of them gave me pleasure; and I may say that though an old man is too often reminded that his friends, like himself, are reaching the end of their earthly probation, I find the waiting period very pleasant, so long as my family circle is intact. *Summum nec metuo diem nec opto.*

The *Evening Standard* has allowed me to reprint articles contributed to that newspaper; Sir John Murray and the Classical Association to reprint the lecture called "Greeks and Barbarians"; and Messrs. Blackwell to reprint the address on "Prayer" read to the Modern Churchmen's Conference last year.

W. R. INGE

BRIGHTWELL MANOR
January 1937

CONTENTS

RELIGION

15

A RUSTIC MORALIST

CONTENTS

ENGLAND

OTHER NATIONS

RELIGION

I

SPECTACLES FOR ALL

I was once asked to reply for the guests at a dinner given by the Worshipful Company of Spectacle Makers. I spoke to the following effect, as far as I can remember.

We ministers of religion are spectacle makers, as you are. Our job is rather more difficult than yours because you help people to see what is visible, while our business is to help people to see the invisible. "The things which are seen are temporal, but the things which are not seen are eternal." But our duty to our patients, penitents, or consultants is the same. They come to us because they cannot see properly. We have to find them a pair of glasses through which they can see properly.

No two people's eyes are exactly alike, and no one person's two eyes are exactly alike. And no one's sight remains exactly the same for more than a few years. It therefore requires a great deal of skill to be an oculist or an optician.

But we have the same trouble in our profession. No two people want exactly the same religion. No one in spiritual matters sees quite straight with both eyes. And no one, in his attitude towards the unseen world, remains exactly where he was ten or twenty years ago.

We all have to live in two worlds. We call them by many different names—the temporal and the eternal, the natural and the spiritual, the visible and the invisible, the world of facts and the world of values, or sometimes, borrowing our imagery from time and space, we talk of the present and the future, or of earth and heaven. We have to cross from one of these worlds to the other constantly, for we have a footing in both, and we need bridges to take us across the chasm which seems to separate them.

Most of what we usually mean by religion—creeds and ritual and sacraments and codes of duties—are bridges of this kind. If they will bear our weight and take us across, that is what we want from them. A "true" bridge is one that serves the purpose of a bridge.

There are of course many people who seldom wish to cross. On one side there are the worldlings, who "mind earthly things," and on the other side there is a small number of contemplative mystics, who are detached from all worldly interests. Both are apt to be indifferent to institutional religion, because they live almost entirely on one or the other side of the gulf. They do not need a bridge to take them across. But the mass of men and women, if they think about spiritual things at all, do need bridges.

The bridge is a good illustration of what religion does for us. My comparison of ministers of religion to spectacle makers may also be helpful. There are some people who seem able to realize the spiritual world without difficulty. They are natural mystics; they have the gift of spirituality. It is a precious gift, like a fine ear for music or a fine taste in art and poetry; but it is not a proof of the highest character.

It is significant that the men whom Christ chose for His apostles were not, if we may judge from the rather dense sayings which are recorded of them, spiritually gifted men. They were brave, loyal, devoted men, true-hearted men. There was not a priest among them.

We have then no right to think poorly of those who are devoid of the mystical sense. Many people are spiritually short-sighted or colour-blind. They try to do their duty, but the inner light burns dimly within them. It is partly temperamental, but very often the cause is simply lack of attention. If we hardly ever try to think about the invisible world, of course it will seem unreal to us. Or there may be some ugly fault in our characters which comes between us and the sight of God.

The large majority, whether they are naturally religious or not, need spectacles, by which I mean all that in my other figure were called bridges. But the Churches cannot provide standardized spectacles for everybody. No two people have exactly the same defect of vision, and as they go through life both their characters and their minds change. The real creed of an old man is not and ought not to be quite the same as that of a young man.

We must test our spectacles for ourselves; no one else can do it for us. A very wise seventeenth-century writer, Whichcote of Cambridge, said: "I will not make a religion for others, nor will I let anyone make a religion for me." Our real religion is what life has taught us.

If you want to know what you really believe, ask yourselves two questions. First, if I had a fairy godmother, who promised me to grant me three wishes, what would those wishes be? Consider this quite seriously. And second, what are the things, if any, that I would die rather than do?

But as I have said, we most of us need spectacles —all that the Churches, all that institutional religion, can provide. They help us to see what we could not see without them. Religious doctrines are not meant to be taken out of their context. They have their proper place in mediating between the two worlds of which I have spoken.

My special point in making this comparison with spectacles is that we cannot have a standardized confession of faith for everybody. We cannot draw up any formulas which will be equally suitable to the learned professor and to his kitchen-maid. The Churches are always making this mistake. They want tests, shibboleths, and they try to make everybody swallow them. Those who refuse are dubbed heretics.

Erasmus long ago protested amusingly against this habit. "It is disgraceful to hurl recklessly at anyone the name of heresy, which is so hateful to Christian ears. But these people are perfectly ready to shout heresy, before they think what they are talking about. And as when one pig grunts, all the rest grunt too, they all join in chorus and say, Down with heresy."

There is plenty of that sort of thing in our day. We are all to wear the standard spectacles, and not to think of providing our own.

If this obvious truth were more generally recognized, that all truth is symbolic, except the highest; that while we live here we all "see through a glass darkly"; and that each man must be allowed to wear the glasses which suit him, we should have much more tolerance and charitableness in religious matters.

The half-educated majority would not storm at the Christian philosopher or man of science, who quite properly tries to harmonize his faith with the convictions to which he has been led by his life's work. And the scholar, on his side, will not think scornfully of the "fundamentalist" or simple believer who finds that the standard spectacles suit him well enough.

We all need such help as we can get, and we need not be ashamed of it. For "to see the invisible" (the phrase comes from the Epistle to the Hebrews) is not a simple matter.

SUBSTITUTES FOR RELIGION

1. Is Religion Declining?

THE general title of this and the articles which are to follow it is taken from an essay by Aldous Huxley. It follows another essay in which he good-humouredly makes fun of me for quoting with approval Professor A. N. Whitehead's words about the essence of religion. "Religion," says this eminent philosopher, "is what the individual does with his own solitude. Collective enthusiasms, revivals, institutions, churches, rituals, Bibles, codes of behaviour, are the trappings of religion, its passing forms. They may be useful or harmful. The end of religion is beyond all this."

Aldous Huxley really agrees with this, for he says that all the founders of the great religions have been solitaries. But if they wished to found popular religions, they failed. "The religions of Jesus, of Gautama, of Lao-Tse, have never appealed to more than a few Christians, Buddhists, Taoists." To satisfy the majority, sociable and unspiritual religions, "formidably rich in all that buys men's souls," had to be invented.

Religions of pure spirituality and solitariness, such as Quakerism, have never been popular. For most people religion is one of the things which a man does not with his solitude, but with his sociableness. We may regret it; but, as Aldous Huxley says, "If the Dean imagines that he is going to transform a single born sociable into a spiritual solitary, he is very much mistaken. Where Buddha and Jesus have failed, will the Dean of St. Paul's and Professor Whitehead of Harvard succeed? I have my doubts."

I have my doubts, too; but I am more than satisfied if what I mean by pure religion is substantially the same as what the Founder of Christianity meant by it. Huxley suggests that I apparently found it easier to pray in my bedroom or study than in St. Paul's. Well, it is true, I did. But I remember a verse in the Sermon on the Mount, and am not ashamed of myself.

All this is just to make it clear what I mean by religion when I ask the question whether religion is declining. For those who think as I do the decay of church-going does not mean the decay of religion. Nor are we much impressed by what many people think encouraging signs—ecstatic revivals in Protestant countries and the crowds who persuade themselves that miracles are worked at Lourdes.

If this last is religion, we may agree with Whitehead that "religion is not always a good thing; it is sometimes a very bad thing." Or, rather, this kind of religion is a very mixed thing; it caters for human nature in all its moods, good and bad,

27

wise and foolish. I do not care much whether this kind of religion increases or declines.

The decline in church-going is easily accounted for. Public worship is indispensable to an illiterate population; but we have, or may have if we want them, masses of good devotional and theological literature. Or we can "listen in"; the B.B.C. is a friend to religion, but no friend to the poor parish priest. The Anglican liturgy is dear to those who were brought up with it, but meaningless in parts to others.

The clergy, it is said, are seldom consulted, and inspire no confidence. There are very many exceptions; but on the whole we must admit that it is true. As long as the idea prevails that the parson is a kind of cheapjack who is paid to cry up certain wares, an advocate who has to speak to his brief, people naturally will not bring their difficulties to him. But if they have reason to think that he is a man who will say only what he believes to be true, whether it is orthodox or not, they will come to him readily enough. We need a new criterion of clerical honesty.

The Church used to get hold of the unconverted by extravagant promises and lurid threats. Organized religion is always directed to the half-converted; this is what Huxley is driving at. But these bribes and threats are heard no more. The clergy are ashamed of them; the people do not believe them. Divine justice must bear some relation to human actions. The natural penalty for being a bad man is not to be baked in an oven; it is to become a worse man, and to banish oneself from the presence of God, here and hereafter.

We hear a great deal about modern "materialism." "Secularism" would be a better word. Materialism is a scientific and philosophical doctrine, which was held by leading men of science in the last century, though they avoided the name. Modern science is not materialistic; but the new ideas, which are still very tentative, will take time to reach the masses. Secularism, however, is another matter. It means the acceptance of a low and unspiritual standard of values, and as such is the deadly enemy of the higher religion. Whether it is increasing or not, it is hard to say. There is certainly far too much of it.

When we turn away from what Whitehead calls the trappings of religion, and look at what he regards as real religion, we should expect, since human nature does not change much, that the number of really religious people probably remains fairly constant. The number is never large, and is never likely to be large. Christ never encourages us to expect an inconvenient crowd on the narrow way. "Few there be that find it." Democracy would like to widen it into an arterial road, but it cannot be done. It will never be safe for motor traffic. There is nothing on which Christ was more explicit than this.

29

But my subject in the articles which are to follow this is to be the various surrogates for religion which now attract numerous disciples. Those who have lost the old beliefs take up various causes, enthusiasms, fads, which promise some satisfaction to their unappeased and often unconscious desires. Most of them are very one-sided and inadequate; they produce fanaticisms, but no real satisfaction.

SUBSTITUTES FOR RELIGION

2. Communism

Those who have studied Communism at close quarters, especially in Russia, seem to agree that it can only be understood as a kind of religion. It has been discussed at the Church Congress as "a rival religion," "a challenge to Christianity." This seems odd when we remember that Lenin described religion as "opium for the people," a noxious drug to be abolished like the traffic in cocaine.

What is meant, of course, is that the symptoms are the same as in the aggressive, epidemic phase of a young religion, Islam for instance. These symptoms are fanatical conviction, enthusiastic propagandism, ruthless persecution of dissentients, and an apocalyptic belief in speedy and complete victory. The symptoms undoubtedly exist. Are they as inexplicable as an epidemic, or can we account for them?

The old political economy was responsible for the figment of the "economic man," against whom Ruskin thundered in vain. The economic man then appeared as a heavy-handed employer of labour. whose prosperity proved the beneficent effects of unrestricted competition. But economic materialism is not necessarily the friend of capitalism. Both sides interpreted history in terms of economics; but the god of one side was the devil of the other. Abstract theories of human nature are apt to lead to violent quarrels, but the economic man has never existed and never will. Life is much more than a livelihood.

It is difficult for those who, like myself, belong to old professional families, to do justice to the Socialist movement. We see the existing system at its best. For generations we have had interesting work, a good social position, moderate and fairly secure incomes, and not very much anxiety. The lot of the English professional man before the war was perhaps the most desirable in the world.

The matter appears differently to those who are exposed to the full blast of cut-throat competition, to fluctuations of trade, to the harassing fear of unemployment, and, if they are employers, to the doubt whether it is possible to succeed in business without sacrificing much that makes life worth living, including perhaps one's conscience as an honest and humane man. Would it not be better for everyone to work for the State, free from wearing anxieties, and secure of a maintenance during good behaviour? Would not this be worth the inevitable loss of liberty, which does not mean much to a large part of the population?

Such arguments may make men socialistic

32

reformers, but not furious fanatics. Communism has a different source. What that source is may be seen easily if we read the literature of the movement. It is sheer hatred.

Hatred is a powerful spur to action, and none the less because it is usually quite irrational. A Corsican family will keep up for generations a vendetta the origin of which has been forgotten. An Irishman would refuse to go to heaven if St. Peter were an Englishman. To excite hatred, it is only necessary to repeat catchwords, the more meaningless the better; they have the same effect that a red rag has on a bull. This art has been carried to perfection in Russia. The Russians are endless and unpractical talkers. When Carlyle spoke of the "strong silent Russians," he was ludicrously wide of the mark.

Can hatred be described as a religious emotion? Unfortunately it can; it has played a great part in religious history. The Jews have always been good haters. "Do not I hate them, O Lord, that hate Thee? Yea, I hate them with a perfect hatred." Even the Apostles wished to call down fire from heaven upon a Samaritan village.

The Communist movement has its bible, like other religions. Its old testament is Hegel, its new testament is Marx on *Capital*. The sacred books are unfortunately chosen, because Hegel was an idealist, who believed that nothing exists except mind. The Communist dogma is that nothing exists except matter. Hegel deified the State, and

C

was accused of teaching that God attained full self-consciousness for the first time in Prussia. Bolshevism has no use for God, conscious or unconscious, and Lenin cared but little for the State. "It is simply the weapon with which the proletariat wages its class-war; a bludgeon, nothing more." The Russians are used to being bludgeoned. Ivan the Terrible and Peter the Great pounded them vigorously; but the little finger of Stalin is thicker than the loins of Peter.

As for the new testament, the works of Marx, Bertrand Russell is right in saying that they belong mentally to the middle of last century. They have no connection with modern economic realities. The class-war is quite out of date in a society like ours, which is rapidly approaching a state of things when there will be no more classes, very few rich men, and several millions of small *rentiers*. The invested savings of the poor since the war are nearly four thousand million pounds. Just at the moment when the capitalist nations are beginning to doubt whether they have taken the wrong road in the over-mechanization of production, the most forbidding aspects of capitalist industry are being introduced into Russia, the worst kind of wage-slavery, without any safeguards at all. Nothing but fanatical hatred could blind so many of the workers of Europe to the real consequences, for their class, of this new "religion."

We need not suppose that any large number of

34

Russians are really convinced. They are terrorized and hypnotized, and the country is hermetically sealed against the entrance of knowledge from outside. The peasants, who began the revolution, are certainly not Communists, and Lenin, with his cynical candour, said that out of every hundred members of the Communist Party one was a genuine Communist, thirty-nine were criminals, and sixty fools.

Hatred is a very poor basis for a religion. It is likely to burn itself away. But it does not follow that this new religion will die out. Religions succeed not because they are true but because they provide what people want; and if people want something different, rather than die, they will change their colour like a chameleon.

Personally, I think that the Russians, who have already substituted State capitalism for Communism, will quietly drop Hegel and Marx, or twist them still further, and revert, with increased zest, to their old policy of territorial expansion. The Germans are honestly convinced that this will happen; and while we are scolding Hitler for his inconvenient activities we ought in fairness to consider what an invasion by a Red army would be like. I am afraid the League of Nations would not be much protection.

SUBSTITUTES FOR RELIGION

3. PATRIOTISM

I MIGHT be tempted to discuss the new nationalist movement on the Continent as the latest development of patriotism. As a substitute for religion, the driving force of the new dictatorships is an intense passion for the country as a unit, the "totalitarian State." In Germany there is even a formal proposal to give up Christianity and return to the worship of the ancient Teutonic gods.

But I think we must not confound what the French call *étatisme*—State-worship—with patriotism. The two overlap, but they are not identical. Most of us in Great Britain love our country dearly, but we certainly do not love the State. The State may be, as Hobbes called it, a Leviathan, a monster which crushes liberty and denies justice to individuals. We may submit to it; we may support it as better than anarchy and disruption; but we cannot possibly love it.

Where any enthusiasm for the State exists, it is either because people have been persuaded into believing in "the group mind," a mystical figment which in practice is only a stick for the backs of minorities, or because the government has skilfully appealed to love of country, while aiming at the sacrifice of the individual to the State, or at power and domination over other States.

Love of country is quite different. Let me say at once that I am not condemning all these "substitutes for religion." They are only wrong when they are exclusive and fanatical. St. Peter sums up our social duties in the words: "Honour all men. Love the brotherhood. Fear God. Honour the King." That is to say, we belong to a number of social organisms, each with a real but limited claim upon us. Besides our primary obligation to God, we are to love our country, and to honour its ruler as representing it. We are to love the brotherhood, that is to say, our fellow Christians. And we are to honour all men. We have duties to the comity of civilized nations, and wider still to all human beings. Sometimes our loyalties may seem to conflict with each other, but we must not evade any of them.

St. Peter's "Honour the King" stands for patriotism, and happily it was easy for us in England to focus our love of country in loyalty, affection, and gratitude to the wise, conscientious, and kindly English gentleman who for twenty-five years reigned over us to our great advantage. It is easy to identify the King with England; no one would regard him as a symbol of "the State."

But we shall understand what we mean by patriotism still better if we compare it with family

37

affection. This comparison has been drawn by the novelist Ernest Raymond in a new book called *What is Patriotism?* edited by N. P. Macdonald. The dry light of reason may assure me that there are probably other women even more richly endowed with all the feminine charms and virtues than my wife, and other children handsomer, cleverer, and not less amiable than my own. But, as Mr. Raymond says, forgetting that he was once a clergyman, "I know it, and I don't care a d——."

There is something faintly humorous in this attitude, as there is in the Englishman's view of life generally. He likes his friends to be as mildly irrational about their wives and families as he is himself. It is just the same about our country. We are often exasperated with our country; we admit that they do some things better in France, or Germany, or America. But we love our country all the same; and it is significant that we think it bad taste to boast of it or praise it, just as we do not boast about our wives.

What is it that I love? Partly the very soil of England. When I look at the meadows, green and gold with fresh grass and buttercups, the tender green of the trees, the white spires of the chestnuts and the delicate pink and white of the apple-blossom, I cannot believe that earth has anything to show more lovable. This love is very near divine worship.

But also I love our national character at its best—

our love of liberty for ourselves and others, our humour and tolerance, our kindliness and fairness. But no, I must not commit the very offence which I have just blamed. Only in my heart of hearts I do agree with the American Santayana: "Never since the heroic days of Greece has the world had such a sweet, just, boyish master."

I know that many great men have roundly abused patriotism. Ruskin calls it "an absurd prejudice founded on an extended selfishness." "A virtue among barbarians," says Havelock Ellis; "a vulgar vice, the collective form of the monopolist instinct," says Grant Allen. It is, in fact, singularly liable to perversion.

It was not an Englishman who said, "My country, right or wrong," and I honestly think that our statesmen and diplomats do not *always* act upon it. But the study of diplomacy is most unedifying reading. Cavour was candid enough to say, "What scoundrels we should be if we did for ourselves the things we are doing for Italy." Bismarck was almost equally unscrupulous; and as long as we have politicians and others who think that morality was only meant for the individual, and has no application to the dealings of nations with each other, we shall never be delivered from the curse of war, which will become more and more ruinous. "I prefer my country to the salvation of my soul," said Machiavelli. This is making patriotism a rival religion indeed. But may not

39

the soul of a nation be lost? And does not *sacro egoismo* come home to roost?

Professor McDougall, the famous psychologist, thinks that there are two standards of ethics, the universal or Christian, and the national or Jewish, and that we cannot do without the second. I do not agree that the Christian standard ruined the Roman Empire, nor that it will ruin any nation that adopts it.

Christ and St. Paul were fervent patriots, but they wished their countrymen to sacrifice their lower ambitions for higher ones, and the Jews could not rise to that magnificent but difficult opportunity. There need be no limit to what our country may mean for us without ceasing to be our country. In a sense, the object of our devotion is "the city of which the type is laid up in heaven," as Plato says, rather than the country which we know and love "in spite of all its faults." It is the same with the Church. St. Paul's "glorious Church, not having spot or wrinkle or any such thing," is not to be found at Rome or Canterbury or Geneva.

As for those superior gentlemen who pride themselves on being free from any patriotic prejudice, I have no respect for them.

SUBSTITUTES FOR RELIGION

4. FASCISM

FASCISM and Nazism were brought into being primarily by the menace of Communism. This vigorous reaction is about all that Bolshevism has effected outside Russia. If this were all, the new dictatorships would naturally pass away when the Communist epidemic subsides into a milder endemic form.

But they have a deeper significance. They are a revolt against the results of the French Revolution, the ideas of 1789. In fact, the French Revolution created, by reaction, nineteenth-century nationalism, just as the Russian Revolution has created the new form of nationalism.

A violent fever generates antitoxins in a healthy body. The French Revolution destroyed a system of hereditary dictatorships and founded bourgeois democracy. Democracy is now being exploded on the Continent by a revival of the old despotic type of government, on a non-hereditary basis, in alliance with the new Socialism, purged, except in Russia, of the element of class-warfare. That is how I see it.

The forms of such a government, whether we

41

call it revolutionary or counter-revolutionary, are prescribed by necessity. The technique of the *coup d'état* is now well understood. If it succeeds it becomes necessary at once to organize the new State so that it may pay its way. Power must be rigidly confined to the victorious faction, and must be concentrated in one man, the dictator. Under him there must be a kind of aristocracy, purely political, recruited with the utmost care and frequently purged from all suspects. It must be supported by a militia which will be the home army, strong enough to crush any rising against the government.

Such a State is rigorously centralized. It can admit no rights of minorities and no popular elections. Every official has authority over his inferiors in the hierarchy, and is responsible only to his superiors.

This looks like a return to the old regime, before 1789. It is so in part, but not entirely. Political democracy has been suppressed, but economic and social democracy is established. It depends on public opinion more than the old monarchies did, and therefore it is obliged to control all the organs which form public opinion.

The liberal and democratic regime of the last century was on principle neutral in religion; it was not interested in Church affairs. Not so the new State, which is anything but neutral in religious matters. It may try to annihilate religion, as in

Russia; or it may proclaim itself Catholic, in the name of the national tradition, as in Italy; or it may attempt to nationalize Christianity, as in Germany.

Liberalism and democracy were secular; the new State, appealing to passionate devotion and loyalty, is necessarily religious, though its religion may take odd forms. The new State, whether in Russia or Italy or Germany, is a religion or a substitute for religion. It is not merely an experiment in government, and it cannot be countered by merely rational arguments.

It is necessarily a danger to Christianity, to peace, and to itself. Christianity is a universal religion; Fascism or Nazism is a national religion. And when two national religions meet, they will fight.

It is dangerous to itself, mainly because it depends so largely on the life of one man. When a dictator dies, his subjects cannot say, "*Le roi est mort: vive le roi.*" The new ruler must be found; and there may be two or three candidates, or none at all. This is really what wrecked the Roman Empire, which became a system of military dictatorships.

An even greater danger, perhaps, is in the probable deterioration in the character of the dictator. The modern State is too complex an affair for any one man to manage, unless he possesses demonic energy and genius, like Napoleon; and such a mind soon burns itself out. Empires die of indigestion, dictatorships of swelled heads.

But I wish to speak of the two chief examples of the new State separately, for they each have interesting features determined by their national history and traditions. I will devote the rest of this chapter to Mussolini and Italy, and reserve Hitler and Germany for my next chapter.

The most remarkable thing about the Italian revolution is its conservatism. It has transformed Italy from within, but it has upset nothing. The King, the Senate, the Chamber of Deputies, universal suffrage, the universities and schools, all remain standing. And yet they are reduced to shadows. Authority comes from above, not from below, and the apex of the pyramid is not the King of Italy, an embarrassed phantom, but the Duce.

His supporters, at any rate when he came into power, were all young men. This is characteristic of all revolutions, and the Great War generated a spirit of impatience and contempt in the minds of the young everywhere.

That Mussolini saved Italy cannot be doubted. Liberalism in Italy had been a dead failure, and the Communists, the traitors of Caporetto, threatened to wreck everything. Mussolini took up the mantle of Mazzini, who was a man of genius under the influence of two ideas, God and nationality. Mussolini captured the revolutionary enthusiasm and turned it into an exalted mystical patriotism.

44

The Duce protests that his new State is for Italy alone. Parliamentary democracy, he has said, may be best for England and France, but not for Italy. The only traditions which Italy possesses are the Roman and the Catholic, both inspired by discipline, hierarchy, authority. (But has he not forgotten medieval Florence and Venice?)

The Fascist State is social rather than political. It recognizes and incorporates syndicalism, capitalism, employers and employed, producers and consumers. Only there must be no idlers and no class enmities. "Each of us," said Rocco, Mussolini's Minister of Justice, "belongs at the same time to several classes." This is the truth which puts Marxism quite out of date. Fascism is indeed far more modern than any other form of government; it has no dogmas, no shibboleths; it is willing to try any experiment.

Its weak point is the romantic dream of reviving the Roman Empire, with Rome as its capital. This dream has given an unhappily militaristic colour to Fascism. Mussolini, who in 1913 declared himself in favour of birth-control, now legislates against it, and offers bribes to fathers of large families, avowedly because Italy needs food for powder, though in reality it is much over-populated. He has already brought Italy into a disgracefully unjust war.

Nevertheless, I have an admiration for the Duce, who is probably the biggest man in Europe.

SUBSTITUTES FOR RELIGION

5. NAZISM

GERMANS have such a genius for putting themselves in the wrong that I am afraid I may only give offence by trying to give a dispassionate sketch of Hitlerism as a substitute for religion. But I can assure my readers that I am neither a Fascist nor a Nazi. I do not approve of concentration camps, or of Jew-baiting, or of sabre-rattling. I only want to understand a movement which has swept a great nation off its feet.

I am neither pro-German nor anti-German. I like fair play and decent generosity. The Germans have not had them, and they are reacting as Germans might be expected to do. Poincaré and Clemenceau are partly responsible for Hitler.

If Mazzini explains Mussolini, Fichte illustrates Hitler. After Napoleon's victories over Prussia at Jena and Auerstadt, the philosopher Fichte roused the Prussians from a state of deep dejection by fervently patriotic lectures, of which this is a specimen:

"From foreign sources Germany has been infected with self-seeking. It must be built up again on a loftier moral plane, for which we require a new system

46

of education. The new education must completely destroy freedom of will. The pupil must not even hear that our impulses and actions may be directed towards our own interests. The foreign genius is like a bee; the German spirit is like an eagle; to have character and to be a German undoubtedly mean the same."

The famous lectures are all like this. The German professors before the war introduced similar boasts into their philosophical and historical lectures, and Hitler and Goering have really surpassed Fichte in bombast.

We, whose humour it is to disparage ourselves, can hardly believe that these rodomontades are not intentional burlesque. But they are not. The Germans were more sincere when they talked about the superiority of their *Kultur* than we were when we pictured England as "the weary Titan," with a mission to educate "the lesser breeds without the law." We never took ourselves very seriously; the Germans did.

Unfortunately, you cannot have delusions of greatness without suffering at the same time from persecution-mania. When I was in Germany in 1911, I found dark suspicions of a plot to "encircle" Germany, and this is still the legend among the Nazis. The bitter humiliation of 1918, which the Germans attribute solely to Communist treachery behind the lines, has only increased this frenzy of self-assertion, which is now a fanatical religion.

47

Nygren, writing on the Church controversy, says: "Race-passion has gone all over Germany; even to many Christians it is so overpowering that it puts Christianity into the shade. The deification of their race is taking the place of religion."

Observe that in Germany it is a deification of *race*. The absurd theory that humanity is at its best only in those of Nordic blood was popularized in Germany by the Frenchman Gobineau and the renegade Englishman Houston Chamberlain.

No one denies that the Nordics are a very fine race; but in point of fact the Germans are less than half Nordic, and are none the worse for a strong infusion of "Alpine" blood. The domed German skull, with no projection at the back, is not Nordic. If we wished to be impolite we might say that an Oriental strain can be detected in not a few Germans. But it was not their fault if the Tartars in the Middle Ages sometimes made free with their women.

These things are obvious to a stranger, but they must not be whispered in Germany. With the supposed object of purifying their national stock they have banished thousands of their ablest citizens.

Goering's *Germany Reborn* is quite delirious about Adolf Hitler. "Just as the Catholic considers the Pope infallible in all matters concerning religion and morals, so do we National Socialists believe with the same inner conviction that the Leader is in all political and social interests of the people simply infallible."

This is military obedience, absolute submission like that of the Jesuits. It is cruel and persecuting; that, unfortunately, is no new thing in fanatical religion. But one cannot read Goering's book, wrong-headed and violent as it is, without a considerable respect for a self-surrender so complete, a love of country so intense. Such men would die for their faith without a moment's hesitation.

I have always thought that if we had offered the Germans terms which they themselves would have thought generous they would have been willing to bury the hatchet.

We did our best to insult and ruin our fallen enemy, and then found, what we ought to have realized at once, that a great nation cannot be trampled on permanently. Of course we were dragged into this course of action by the French; but we are used to French dictation in these days.

The strong point in Nazism is the abolition of class-jealousies. From all accounts, the employers and employed fraternize in Germany as they never did before. When we remember the extreme bitterness of German Socialism this is a great achievement. The people are really in good heart, after many years of despair and misery. And they have made a great effort to clean up certain unsavoury corners of their moral stable, which had long been a reproach to German civilization.

Sir Austen Chamberlain and many others think that they are threatening the peace of Europe. With their traditions they could not recover their self-respect without a strong army. And they are by no means secure against attack either on their eastern or western front.

It is useless to accuse them of breach of treaties. Disarmament was never meant to be unilateral; either all must disarm or none.

I shall be sorry if this new substitute for religion goes on much longer. A nation in which freedom of thought and speech has been suppressed cannot play its proper part in the common task of civilized humanity, and what priceless contributions Germany has made in the past to philosophy, learning, science, literature and music!

A dictator cannot even tell what people are thinking. If he puts his ear to the ground he hears only the echo of his own voice. But what will follow Nazism I cannot even guess. The fate of all Europe depends on the preservation of peace.

SUBSTITUTES FOR RELIGION

6. BUSINESS

LONG ago, when Mr. Holloway of the Pills died, his obituary notice in *The Times* contained the following remarkable passage: "Money-making is an art by itself; it demands for success the devotion of the whole man. Sleeping or waking his thoughts must be devoted to it. It is not everyone who is capable of such single-hearted attention as this. Most men wish to be wealthy, but with a want of steadiness and singleness of purpose. Politics or love are great things to them; they are not willing to give them up just as so many snares by which the path of money-making is beset."

We cannot serve God and Mammon, as a great authority told us two thousand years ago, when trade and commerce were very simple affairs compared with what they are to-day. Mammon, the writer of the obituary notice agrees, is as exacting a master as his rival.

Samuel Butler characteristically says that no doubt it is difficult to serve both; but everything that is worth doing is difficult. Is it only difficult, or is it impossible?

The money-making life has not always been held

up to admiration. The Greeks thought it a legitimate career, but not one that an educated gentleman would care for. The early Church held the curious view that money is "naturally barren," so that there is something unnatural in making it breed. The Jews, of course, made it breed, but they were not Christians. The Christian noble, if he wanted money, might set up as a robber baron, or

> By way of mild reminders
> That he needed coin, the knight
> Day by day extracted grinders
> From the howling Israelite.

There were prosperous merchants in the Middle Ages, and they were respected. But the modern business man has his spiritual home in Calvinism, which has had a very important influence upon the social and economic state of Europe.

The Church hitherto had not been quite easy in its mind about private property. If man had not fallen into sin, there would be no law, no armies, and no private property. These institutions belong not to the absolute Law of Nature, but to the relative Law of Nature, which we have to accept only because we are in a fallen state.

But Calvin swept away this distinction; private property now becomes, without qualification, part of the divine law. He was convinced that Christianity is compatible with industrialism and capitalism, and that this type of civilization is, or

52

may be, more Christian than the feudalism and militarism of the Middle Ages.

He wished his adherents to lead a strict, disciplined, self-denying life, without following the Catholic tradition of the elders, with its arbitrary rules about fasting and penance. So he taught that productive labour, and abstinence from all needless self-indulgence, are the typical godly life.

I do not think he foresaw the inevitable effect of his teaching. But it is plain that if you can convince a whole nation that steady industry is eminently pleasing to God, and that almost all ways of spending money unproductively are wrong, that nation is likely to become very prosperous.

We must not suppose that Calvin was blind to the abuses of money-making; on the contrary he condemned them severely. Every kind of fraud and dishonesty, every kind of speculation, every kind of oppression, came under his lash.

Do not let us despise the Puritans; we should be better for a considerable infusion of Puritanism in our post-war society.

The defects of Calvin's scheme would have been apparent earlier but for the old political economy of the nineteenth century. We were invited to admire the beautiful harmony and automatic working of the economic system, which provided an easy road from "each for self" to "each for all." It would be futile to resist the "natural laws" laid down by the Divine Legislator. So with a good conscience men took what they could get, and the devil took the hindmost.

But the Puritan social order broke up from within. Big Business ceased to be ascetic; it ceased to be religious; it ceased to be honest. The manufacturer was displaced by the banker, the banker by the mere brigand, the Napoleon of finance.

To "make" money now meant to acquire it, no matter how. The best method has been by securing a monopoly, and those who care to do so may study the tactics of (for example) the Standard Oil Trust. The great American fortunes read like a *reductio ad absurdum* of capitalism.

Carnegie was one of the best of the millionaires, for he made his money in trade; but the story of his retirement from business gives food for thought. Pierpont Morgan said to his associate, Schwab, "If Andy wants to sell, I'll buy. Go and find his price." Schwab went, and after a few minutes' talk Carnegie wrote on a piece of paper, "Four hundred million dollars." Morgan at once accepted, and shook hands with Carnegie with the words, "Mr. Carnegie, I want to congratulate you on being the richest man in the world."

Can we wonder that men are beginning to think that there must be something radically wrong with a system under which this sort of thing is possible?

I have called it a substitute for religion. This does not apply to such types as Jay Gould, but it does apply to many successful men in the nineteenth century, and to a few even now.

Bertrand Russell quotes Rockefeller as saying to his Bible class: "It is wrong to assume that men of immense wealth are always happy. If a man lives his life for himself and has no regard for humanity he will be the most miserable man on earth. The kind of man I like is one that lives for his fellows, contented with his lot, and trying to bestow all the good he can on humanity."

Lippmann says: "The sponsors of the Broadway Temple in New York proclaimed a campaign to buy bonds as a five per cent investment in your fellow man's salvation." The five per cent was based on Christian grounds and on gilt-edged mortgage.

A very mild echo of this smug complacency may be found in Smiles's *Self-Help*, a favourite gift to boys when I was young. Christ speaks of those who "strain at a gnat and swallow a camel." He has another saying about a camel, too.

It is strange that there should be no limit to acquisitiveness, considering that nature has given us only one stomach. As the medieval jingle says, *Non est in mundo dives qui dicit abundo.* The Communists think they can destroy covetousness by a radical operation. Remove the temptation and the vice will disappear.

But even if "the World" could be scotched, the Flesh and the Devil remain, and acquisitiveness

55

will return under another form. The mere bandit must be dealt with by the law.

For ordinary mortals we must trust to removing the prestige which still attaches to mere wealth, and I think there has been a great change in this direction within my lifetime. The mere collector of stocks and shares is what the New Testament calls him, a fool.

SUBSTITUTES FOR RELIGION

7. SUPERSTITION

THERE are many things in our civilization which
can only be understood if we remember that, in
spite of our amazing progress in scientific knowledge—confined, however, to a very few persons—
and in the arts which minister to comfort, we are
descended from a long line of savages, who have
transmitted to us their characters almost unaltered.
Our civilization is not even skin-deep; it reaches
no lower than our clothes. Humanity is still essentially Yahoo-manity.

Our superstitions are the symptoms of a racial
disease from which we are slowly recovering, a
disease which has inflicted more misery on mankind
even than war. The lives of barbarians are plagued
by superstition, and Europe remained on this side
thoroughly barbarous till quite modern times.

The history of sorcery and witchcraft is the most
ghastly chapter in all the records of the past, and,
strangely enough, the most atrocious cases belong
to the period of the Renaissance and after.

Seven thousand (says Lecky) were burned for
sorcery at Trèves, six hundred by a single bishop
at Bamberg, nine hundred in one year at Wurtz-

burg. At Toulouse the Inquisition burned four hundred at once; five hundred witches perished at Geneva in three months; a thousand in one year at Como.

One country was as bad as another, and the scandal went on for centuries. A sorcerer was burned in Spain in 1780, and another in France in 1718.

The latest victim of the superstition was an English doctor in Uganda, who was nearly killed by a pious native Christian. The good man had found in his Bible, "Thou shalt not suffer a witch to live," and in his language there is one word for "medicine-man" and "witch."

The attitude of the Catholic Church in encouraging these judicial massacres was detestable. But the Protestants were almost, if not quite, as bad. Among the staunch believers in witchcraft were Luther, Baxter, and (alas!) John Wesley.

Under the Commonwealth sixty persons were hanged for witchcraft in Suffolk in one year. We are told that the English laws were "far milder" than those on the Continent. Our usual methods were to prick the suspected persons all over with needles, to throw them into the water to see whether they would float (if they did they were witches), and to keep them awake by prodding them for five or more nights.

If these gentle methods extorted confession the culprits were usually hanged, not burned. In Scotland the most frightful instruments of torture were applied for several days in succession. The astonishing thing is that hardly anyone pitied the victims, most of whom were harmless old women.

Superstition manufactures its own evidence, and the evidence is, or appears to be, cogent. We shall not understand its great strength unless we constantly bear this in mind. The commonest charge against witches was of smiting married men with impotence. When the witch was duly burned, the husband recovered. It is, of course, notorious now that this condition is usually the result of nervousness; but many thousands of poor old women died in torments on this accusation. Others suffered on the charge of keeping devils as lovers or mistresses

Superstition has seen its best, or worst, days. In its surviving forms it is silly rather than horrible, but it is none the less discreditable.

The royal touch as a cure for scrofula was believed in for centuries. The service for the ceremony may be found in the prayer-books of Queen Anne. Charles II touched nearly one hundred thousand persons. But it went out with the Stuarts. William III reluctantly consented to perform the rite, but his comment was "I wish you better health and more sense."

The evil eye is one of the most universal of all superstitions. In parts of Italy, and in the south of Europe generally, it is unwise to say, "What a pretty child!" in the hearing of its parents, unless you add, "May God preserve it." In Ireland it is said that some of the peasants still believe that their priests can turn them into rats.

Equally ancient and universal are superstitions about dreams, and many people in this country still believe them. I shall make the psycho-analysts furious (since they consider themselves nothing if not scientific) when I say that the absurd importance which many of them give to dreams may perhaps be traced to this ignoble source.

An unutterably silly superstition is that against sitting down thirteen to dinner. I suppose this is connected with the Last Supper. I have sometimes been astonished to find persons whose intelligence was not otherwise contemptible the victims of this superstition. Most London hostesses will put themselves to serious inconvenience if the fourteenth dinner-guest fails to appear.

Those who study the births, deaths, and marriages in the newspapers must have noticed that marriages almost cease in the month of May. Tennyson says, "In the spring a young man's fancy lightly turns to thoughts of love," but apparently the young man must wait till June before enjoying the happiness of the married state.

I once had a West End parish, with a highly educated congregation, and I was so much irritated by this absurd fashion that I preached a sermon about superstition, telling them politely not to be such fools, and asking them whether they really supposed that God was the kind of person to punish them for getting married in one month rather than another.

They told me they supposed it had something to do with the Virgin Mary. In point of fact, the superstition is much older. It is mentioned as an old custom by Ovid, who naturally knew nothing of the Virgin Mary. He suggests that the uncanny festival called Lemuralia occurs in May, and that this may be the reason why marriages in that month are "forbidden."

I may add that my wife and I were married in May, and in thirty-two years nothing very dreadful has happened to either of us.

Is all this play or earnest, or something between the two, an indulgence given to subconscious race-habits, which were once desperately serious? The last, I think. We sometimes play at being savages, and it is not so entirely play as we pretend. "There may be something in it"; so we behave as if we thought there was something in it.

We ought not to do it. We cannot really be Christians till we have banished the relics of savage religion from our minds. In Southern Europe the priests unhappily exploit superstition. It is the line of least resistance; but for a true minister of Christ the line of least resistance is always the wrong line. And I am sure we ought to be careful not to put these foolish ideas into the minds of our children.

II—*continued*

SUBSTITUTES FOR RELIGION

8. CRANK BELIEFS

THE crank is an Anglo-Saxon product; he flourishes in Great Britain and in the United States, and is rare everywhere else. In the Latin countries he hardly exists. The Mediterranean lands have a longer tradition of civilization; their people are more sophisticated and perhaps better educated. They do not commit themselves to absurd fads.

But we in England have always encouraged, or at least not repressed, originality and eccentricity. The French say we have two hundred religions and only one sauce—which is perhaps better than having two hundred sauces and no religion.

The United States is the happy hunting-ground of freak religions. Their exports to this country include not only duchesses and chewing-gum, but Christian Science, spiritualism, the group movement, and many other suchlike things, some of which take as kindly to our climate as the musquash and the Colorado beetle.

Santayana, whose *Soliloquies in England* is the most sympathetic, most understanding, and wittiest study of our character, manners, and customs that I know, says that our country is the paradise of individuality, eccentricity, heresy, anomalies, hobbies, and humours. "Where else would a man inform you, with a sort of proud challenge, that he lived on nuts, or was in correspondence through a medium with Sir Joshua Reynolds, or had been disgustingly housed when last in prison?"

The Englishman always rides some hobby. He travels through the world with one eye shut, hops all over it on one leg, and plays his scales with one finger. He will defend the silliest opinion with a mint of learning, and espouse the worst of causes on the highest principles.

The crank belief may be a substitute for religion when it takes on the properties of a religious dogma. The belief may have nothing in common with religion except its quality of absoluteness. There is a recognizable crank mind which when it has picked up an idea turns it into a sacred conviction and tries to propagate it with the fanatical zeal of a bigot.

Some content themselves with one craze; others drive a whole team of them. There are some men, often half in and half out of politics, who may be described as the "antis." They are anti-vaccination, anti-vivisection, anti-corporal punishment, anti-alcohol, anti-tobacco, and so forth.

In the early days of Christianity the only craze of this kind was anti-sex. Some of the hermits and monks brought themselves into such a state that the sight of a pretty girl made them feel sick, just as the smell of beer or tobacco turns the stomach of the fanatical teetotaller or anti-smoker.

The worst of the crank is that he takes it as a personal insult if you do not agree with him. He is the most alarming of bores. He is also the terror of candidates for Parliament. These unfortunate gentlemen have not only to echo like parrots the shibboleths of the party programme for the time being; they have to promise, on pain of losing the votes of this or that clique, to vote for the abolition of vaccination, vivisection, capital punishment, birth-control, field-sports, gambling, and what not.

Some of these "causes" may be good; but what must be the state of mind of a voter who is willing to make any one of them decide his political allegiance? This is the way to rot democracy.

No doubt it may be said that no reforms would ever be carried out if there were not a few unbalanced enthusiasts who think that this particular reform is the one thing that must be pushed through at all costs.

Was not St. Paul considered a crank by educated pagans? Were not St. Francis and George Fox men of one idea, and very unlike ordinary people? This is, of course, the plea and the partial justification of what in the eighteenth century was called enthusiasm; but one cannot seriously compare such men as these with the monomaniacs who believe that the British are the lost ten tribes, or that "millions now alive will never die." (A few years ago this announcement appeared on thousands of posters.)

It gives one a sense of insecurity to know that the destinies of the country are in the hands of persons of such low intelligence. But, fortunately, the crank is only insane at one point. In other ways we often find him quite sensible.

Many of us keep our ideas very comfortably in watertight compartments. There is, perhaps, not much danger that any one fad will sweep the country. Prohibition in America was a war measure; its advocates took advantage of an exceptional crisis; and now at last it has been repealed.

Nothing has damped the ardour of teetotal fanatics like the temporary success and ultimate failure of their propaganda in the United States. And yet theirs is one of the most respectable of all crazes, for drunkenness used to be a terrible evil. The demon was exorcized, not by the cranks, but by better education and increasing refinement. I wish I could hope that the same influences would eventually drive out betting and gambling and other follies.

Why is it that we so seldom hear of these fanatically supported "causes" in Roman Catholic countries? One reason I have given already; but also, the idea that religion consists in getting things done is a Protestant notion. Catholicism understands human nature too well to indulge in the queer *naïveté* of the Protestant social reformer. On the other hand it will seldom reform an abuse unless the interests of the Church are concerned. I suppose we must take the rough with the smooth and allow our geese to cackle. They once saved the Capitol at Rome by giving the alarm, according to the old story. Their descendants have never forgotten it.

III

PRAYER

I AM asking you to consider the subject of Prayer. I think I must assume, at least for the purposes of our study, that each of you engages in private prayer as a daily habit, and could not imagine how any religion could subsist without it; and that we all at times feel perplexed as to what prayer actually is and does.

There is no subject on which Christ spoke with more downright explicitness than on the efficacy of prayer. "All things whatsoever ye shall ask in prayer, believe that ye receive them and ye shall have them." "Whatsoever ye shall ask the Father in my name, He shall give it you." "Everyone that asketh receiveth."

These very definite promises seem to be contradicted by common experience. Most of us would say that they have been contradicted by our own experience. Hence the problem which troubles us all at times. It is a vital question, for if prayer has no efficacy we must give up not only our trust in the plain words of Christ, but all practice of religion. For if prayer has no result, no one would care to pray; and without prayer there can be no religion. Prayer is the very breathing of religion, its most essential and characteristic activity.

67

Let us then ask ourselves what prayer is in itself. It is the mystical act *par excellence*, and is common to all religious persons, even the most unmystical. It consists of a lifting up of the soul to God (this definition, usually ascribed to St. Thomas Aquinas, is really as old as St. Basil). A lifting up of the soul to God; that is one side of it; and a descent of the Spirit of God into the human soul; that is the other side of it. If either of these is absent, there is no true prayer. The Johannine Christ clearly lays down the condition for effectual prayer. "If ye abide in me, and my words abide in you, ye shall ask what ye will and it shall be done unto you." As St. Paul says, "The Spirit makes intercession for us," and "helps our infirmities." Wherever there is true prayer it consists of these two elements and no others.

Dr. Matthews has pointed out that there can be no true prayer except to a God who is both immanent and transcendent. A purely immanent Deity, indistinguishable from our own best selves, is not a possible object of adoration, and adoration, as von Hügel and others have insisted, is the supreme act in prayer. On the other side, if God were purely transcendent, no communion with Him would be possible. God is infinitely far above us, and yet we can commune with Him. This can only be if the Spirit of God prays in us. Not all prayers, of course, are so inspired; but those that are not "never to heaven go," as the King in

Hamlet says. The thought that in real prayer the Holy Spirit is actually bearing witness with our spirit, praying with, through, and for us is infinitely solemn, and we dare not forget the warnings that that divine presence can dwell only in a purified heart. We may grieve the Spirit, we may quench the Spirit, in the last resort we may even blaspheme against the Spirit. Dryness in prayer is not always a penalty, but often it is; and it is not our state of mind while we are on our knees that is responsible for it, but what has gone before.

This conception of prayer is both wider and narrower than the popular idea of what prayer is. It rules out many unhallowed petitions in which the Spirit of God has no part. But it includes much that is not petition at all. If our prayers are entirely or almost entirely petitions, they fall very short of what all the masters of the spiritual life tell us that prayer ought to be. Thanksgiving, intercession, meditation, contemplation, adoration, and orison or silent prayer, are all enumerated as parts of prayer. Those who have found the silent yearning of the soul, which is in truth a preparation of the channels through which grace is to flow, the most fruitful method of prayer, can appeal to many authorities; but I think the use of set forms, morning and evening, ought not to be discontinued. I strongly recommend the beautiful old office of compline for our evening prayer, at bed-time.

The old proverb, *Laborare est orare*, and Hegel's

Das Denken ist auch Gottesdienst, extend the province of prayer still further. If we remember St. Paul's words, "Whether ye eat or drink or whatsoever ye do, do all to the glory of God"; if we perform the duties of our daily round sacramentally, as it were, then our activity may be called an acted prayer, even though the mind may not at the time be turned directly to thoughts of God. Here it will be seen that we have departed far from the idea that prayer is merely petition.

If we ask next, why do men pray? the simple answer is, because they cannot help it. Man has always been a praying creature, though in primitive societies prayer is extremely crude and super-stitious. In this case, as in almost every other, we must observe Aristotle's canon that the *nature* of anything is its complete development. By their fruits, not by their roots, we shall know them. Prayer is born of two opposite states of mind, the sense of alienation from the unseen Power which surrounds us and controls our fate, and the desire for communion with it. We desire to know the will of God, to understand and co-operate with Him, not blindly to oppose Him. We desire to open out our hearts and minds that He may fill them. This desire, and the effort to which it gives rise, is spontaneous and natural; it is its own justification and satisfaction. It is justified, and it brings satis-faction, because, as St. Augustine says in the most familiar words he ever wrote, "Thou, O God, hast made us for Thyself, and our hearts are unquiet until they rest in Thee." The spiritual world is there all the time, encircling and penetrating us. And it is something more than an atmosphere. The word personality is no doubt very inadequate to describe the nature of God; He is not a Person among other persons. But His nature is not *less* than personal; if we think of Him as impersonal we are limiting Him still more. Especially in prayer, the best way is to think of Him quite simply as One who hears what we say, and sometimes gives us an answer which we think we can recognize as an answer. But we cannot always draw a line between the prayer and its answer. It is a common mistake to wait for and expect some irruption of the divine into our hearts which we can recognize as not our own. That is not the normal way in which the divine Spirit acts upon us. On the Godward side the gates of personality are always open. God redeems and saves us by imparting Himself to us; by changing our wills, enlightening our understandings, and quickening our affections.

In so far as prayer is loving intercourse or reverent homage, or thanksgiving, or meditation on the revealed attributes of God, or contrition for sin, it is meaningless to ask whether it is efficacious. No one doubts that as an exercise it deepens the character, strengthens the will, purifies the affections, and brings peace, rest, and blessedness. These things are not in dispute. We in this Society

71

have no wish to shirk any real difficulties, and I do not mean to shirk them. But I have thought it worth while to emphasize that when we discuss the efficacy of prayer in the narrow sense in which the phrase is commonly used, we are not dealing with prayer as a whole, or raising any questions about the value of a habit of prayer. That prayer in the wider sense is valuable we all admit. It is only a particular kind of effect, which has been supposed to follow from a particular kind of prayer, which is in dispute.

Let us go back to the words of Christ. They certainly seem to promise that our petitions, of whatever kind, will be granted if made in the name of Christ. Many children, and perhaps some grown people, think that if we add to our petitions, "through Jesus Christ our Lord," or "for Jesus Christ's sake," God has promised to grant them. We are allowed to use the name of Christ as a man might use the name of a friend to back a bill. To this there is a plain answer. To a Jew the name of God means more than a mere appellation. Many passages in the Old Testament make this clear. It is not a quibble to say that in the name of Christ means in the spirit of Christ, to pray as He prayed. And when we think, for example, of His prayer in the garden of Gethsemane, we observe three things; first, that the prayer was for deliverance from physical suffering; next, that it was conditional on its being in accordance with the will of God;

and finally, that it was not granted in the literal
sense. The same may be said of St. Paul's petition
to be relieved from the "stake in the flesh." Further,
we may remember the prohibition of vain repeti-
tions in the Sermon on the Mount, with the reason
given. "Your Father knoweth what things ye have
need of before ye ask Him."

There has been a change in our time towards
greater caution and diffidence in petition. We pray
with less assertiveness than our grandparents did,
and probably on an average we pray less than they
did, at any rate for earthly favours. The coroner
who directed his jury to bring in a verdict of "died
by act of God," if they could find no "rational
explanation" of the death, represented a way of
thinking which is much less common than it used
to be. The old dualism of natural and supernatural,
of law and miracle, which is still maintained over
a great part of Christendom, is increasingly unwelcome to us. The notion that the world is governed
by natural laws which may be suspended or modified at any time by divine intervention, is felt to be
one of the least satisfactory of philosophies. This
change has inevitably altered our conception of
the nature of prayer. Old-fashioned exhortations
about "wrestling Jacob" and "besieging the mercy-
seat" are seldom now applied to petitions for earthly
blessings.

Emerson speaks of the childlike confidence in
the compelling power of prayer which he had met

73

with in his youth. "The minister at Sudbury being at the Thursday lecture at Boston heard the officiating clergyman praying for rain. As soon as the service was over he went to the officiating minister and said, 'You Boston ministers, as soon as a tulip wilts under your windows, go to church and pray for rain, until all Concord and Sudbury are under water.'" Not long ago, during an eruption of Mount Etna, the inhabitants of the village of Castiglione, preceded by their priest, carried a wonder-working image of St. Egidio to the place of danger, and adjured the lava to change its direction and flow towards the neighbouring village of Linguaglossa. The people of Linguaglossa, having no miraculous image, resorted to the arm of flesh. The combatants were separated by the police. We cannot pray like this now: it seems to us both wrong and foolish. As long as it was doubtful whether an outbreak of cholera in a town was caused by an infected water-supply or by the blasphemies of an infidel mayor, science was paralysed. Even the prayers in the Prayer Book for rain and fine weather are seldom used, and are rather disliked by an educated congregation. We know that the medicine-men in savage Africa are in request as rain-makers, and that this superstition is not quite extinct even in Europe; but we should be ashamed to believe it.

Are we then not to pray for earthly things at all? That is not St. Paul's advice. "In everything, by prayer and supplication with thanksgiving, let your bequests be made known unto God." To make our wishes known, and to demand that they shall be gratified, are different things. The more we know about the causes of climatic phenomena, the less likely we are even to dream of changing them in order to save our hay-crop, or to secure a fine day for our garden-party.

But can we consistently give up praying for rain with the expectation of altering the weather for our benefit, and continue to pray for the recovery of a relation or friend in sickness? Knowledge has been enlarged in this field also during our lifetime. We know something about microbes; how can they be affected by our prayers? Some of you may remember that a controversy was once carried on in two monthly reviews about the efficacy of prayer. It was proposed to test the external value of prayer by experimenting on hospital patients. The occupants of one ward of a hospital were to be the subjects for a stated period of special intercession by a large body of the faithful, while those in the other wards were to be left to the general prayers of the Church. A comparison of the death-rates would, it was suggested, decide once for all whether special prayers have any effect or not. The controversy was not conducted in a very edifying manner. The spokesmen on the orthodox side expressed great indignation, and seemed to evade what was really a perfectly fair and plain question, namely, Does prayer have any external effect such as can be measured by statistical methods? Supposing that those who offered petitions for the recovery of the patients in the selected ward were not actuated by any wish to "tempt God"—supposing that they were animated by pure and simple faith—supposing that all the conditions for prevailing prayer were fulfilled—would any result follow of which a physician or a life-insurance company ought to take notice? Is the husband of a loving and prayerful wife a "better life," from the point of view of life-insurance, than a man who has no Christian relatives anxious for the prolongation of his existence? These are questions which a man may surely ask without impiety, and they are questions which a statistical inquiry alone could answer. I would go further and say that they are questions on which a Christian ought to have some opinion. I suppose I should be right in saying that the teaching of old-fashioned Evangelicals, both in the Anglican Church and outside it, was decidedly in favour of the belief that prayer can alter events; and I believe that many would shrink from an impartial test, because they wish to believe that it does, but are afraid that their belief would not stand investigation.

Let me then say candidly that I do not believe that the result of such an investigation would be agreeable to the old-fashioned believer. Of course I put aside considerations which appear to me to be evasive, such as the encouragement given to the sufferer by knowing that his friends were praying for him. We want to know whether any direct external influence can be traced. And I fear that, as a matter of experience, it cannot.

The deterministic argument against prayer does not seem to me conclusive. It may be that all consequences are indissolubly linked to their antecedents; but still it does not follow that prayer cannot be an efficient cause. If God foreknew the microbes, He also foreknew the prayer. Both alike are part of the warp and woof out of which the world's history is woven. We cannot say offhand that there is and can be no connection between the course of the disease and the prayer that the disease may take a favourable turn. It is, I think, a matter which must be decided by evidence, and I believe the evidence is negative.

If we face this fairly and without evasive reservation, we shall then be able to ask ourselves whether we would really have it otherwise. The answer will depend a good deal on what we believe about pain and death. It is not only Christian Scientists who find the existence of suffering in the world a greater trial to their faith than the existence of sin. There are many who think that if God is good it cannot be His will that His creatures should suffer and die. Well, Christianity is surely at one with science in holding that death is as natural and beneficent as life, being in fact the necessary condition of the renewal of life and youth in the world. All things that are born have but a short time to live, and then they turn again to their dust. This is God's law; why should we rebel against it? "Into the breast that gives the rose shall I with shuddering fall?" "Glad did I live and gladly die, and I laid me down with a will." Nor is it natural or possible that all creatures shall live out their span of life. There is nothing shocking in early death; "whom the gods love die young." I cannot think that even when we are in agonized anxiety we should really wish to play Providence. I think that at such times most of us are really content to repeat the prayer of Christ, "Father, if it be possible let this cup pass from me; nevertheless, not as I will but as Thou wilt." There is here no attempt, no wish, to control events or to alter His wise and merciful will.

If we think that we should like to control events by our prayers, let us consider how we should like the idea of our neighbour being able to control them by his. I once had a letter from a good lady who said, "I am praying for your death. I have been very successful in two other cases."

If then we frankly give up the desire to alter physical laws, what are we to say about prayer for spiritual things? We think that spiritual law is less rigorous; but is this only our ignorance? If we knew all, should we find the same inexorable law as in the physical world? This is a difficult question. But I believe myself that the laws of

78

spirit are different. I believe that the system under which we live is not a soulless mechanism, but a great system of ends—a system of vital purposes which have a freedom and elasticity far greater than the analogy of the natural sciences would lead us to suppose. Nature appears mechanical because it is uniform; but how if the uniformity be due simply to the steadiness and even operation of the divine will, which does not need to change because it never makes a mistake? Natural law is God's way of doing things. If a clock goes uniformly, we do not assume that it made itself, whereas a clock that goes badly and needs shaking and altering the hands gives evidence of a conscious mind. I have already said that as a matter of evidence I do not believe in special providences and miracles wrought by prayer in the field of nature. But when we come to spirit the evidence seems to be the other way, and I attach no value to *a priori* arguments against it. It is the old puzzle of determinism and free will—very perplexing theoretically, but not practically.

The soul grows and expands under a regime of prayer as the body under a course of good food and exercise. And though in praying for earthly blessings we may think it better to reduce mere petition to a minimum, in praying for spiritual graces we do ask fervently that something may be given us. We may do so without scruple, because we know that "this is the will of God, even our sanctification."

In praying for the gifts of the Spirit, we know that He to whom we pray inspires the prayer, and can grant it, for what we are asking Him to give us is Himself. And I doubt if anyone who has made a practice of this kind of prayer has ever given it up because he has found it useless.

The question about intercession for spiritual graces to be granted to others is not quite so easily answered. But I am far from thinking that such prayers are necessarily unavailing. The mysteries of personality are unfathomable. In the psychology of St. Paul's Epistles, which has been the Christian psychology generally, while the life of the *psyche* seems to be purely individual, that of the *pneuma* seems to be super-individual; "we are all made to drink into one Spirit." I certainly do not think that we need do violence to our natural instincts by refusing to pray for others, or to doubt that our prayers may really help them.

Let me sum up what I have been saying by a few aphorisms.

Providence does not begin where nature leaves off.

Things are not specially "providential" because they suit our convenience.

It is God's will that His creatures should have many troubles to bear, and that they should die.

If the order of nature is not broken by so-called supernatural interventions, the probable reason is that the Author of nature is satisfied with the regular operation of His own laws.

"He who rises from his knees a better man, his prayer has been granted." This is from George Meredith, who no doubt believed that the value of prayer is purely subjective. But it is a good saying, as far as it goes.

"Prayer is the elevation of the mind (or soul) to God." Do not be content with any narrower definition, and remember that this act of recollection may be performed at any time, and should always be performed when we are beginning any new task. The soldier's prayer in going into action, "Lord, if at any time to-day I forget Thee, do not Thou forget me," is a good model.

"If we ask anything according to His will, He heareth us." But the answer may be, "My grace is sufficient for thee, for my strength is made perfect in weakness."

"This is the will of God, even your sanctification."

IV

THE ESTABLISHED CHURCH

Now that the whole nation has been listening to and taking part in the beautiful, dignified, and moving obsequies of a beloved King, we may fairly call attention to the grievous loss which on all such occasions would be felt if we ceased to be officially a Christian country.

On January 28th, we realized that we are a Christian country, and that the Church of England should at such times act as the national Church.

I do not think that at the funeral of King George any jealousy was felt by other Churches. When representing the nation the Established Church is no sect, but the spokesman of all "who love the Lord Jesus Christ with sincerity." If the Church were disestablished, not only would all the stately and reverent ceremonial which seems to be increasingly valued by our countrymen be lost on occasions of public mourning and thanksgiving, but its leaders would be unable to speak, as they now can, in the name of English Christianity.

There was, I imagine, no Free Churchman who did not feel that the Archbishop of Canterbury, whose tributes to the late King were marked by such perfect taste and such deep feeling, was expressing admirably the minds of all Christians.

In Europe, as it is now, the idea of a national Church is right and natural. A co-ordinated system of national Churches, not enslaved to the State, not accepting the State as the ultimate authority in spiritual matters, but representing the State on the religious side, is the type of ecclesiastical organization proper to our time.

The ancient notion of a universal political Church, corresponding to a universal political empire, was obsolete long before Napoleon gave the *coup de grâce* to the Holy Roman Empire, which was neither holy nor Roman nor an empire.

What do we mean when we speak of an established Church? Ever since Augustine of Canterbury (about A.D. 600) Church and State in England have been closely connected. Every member of the Church was a member of the State, and every member of the State was by right a member of the Church.

These are two aspects of an indivisible unity. To this day we pray for the King, "over all persons and in all causes, ecclesiastical as well as civil, in these his dominions supreme." The King symbolizes the indivisible unity of the Christian State.

It will, of course, be said that this theory no longer corresponds with the facts, because we are not all Churchmen or even Christians. We are not all patriots either, except when we are deeply stirred; but at such times we rediscover our unity, both in civil and spiritual matters.

83

What would be the consequences if, as Bishop Creighton said, we repudiated the Christian basis of the State? What is the "establishment" against which voices are raised, even by disgruntled Churchmen? The Crown never claimed spiritual jurisdiction, except for twenty years in the sixteenth century. It protected the rights and property of the Church, made them "stable." The parochial system was recognized and supported by the law of the land.

In every parish there was a person, or "parson," to whose services every inhabitant of the district had a legal right. All have a right to worship in the parish church, to be baptized, married, and buried within its precincts. There are some districts where Free chapels or churches have had to be closed; the Anglican clergyman cannot run away if he wishes to do so.

I do not think I am prejudiced when I say that, in the villages especially, the presence of a resident clergyman has been of immense value.

We sometimes hear from Episcopalians in Wales, Scotland, and the Dominions that they are content to be disestablished. But they derive prestige, though they are in a small minority, from having a big brother behind them.

Discontented Churchmen sometimes complain of Crown appointments. In the eighteenth century and the early part of the nineteenth century there were scandals, though nothing that the

Crown ever did was so bad as the unblushing nepotism of the bishops themselves.

But at present there are no scandals and very few bad appointments. There are just a few clergymen, I regret to say, who sit on the steps of 10 Downing Street and ask for bishoprics; but they very seldom get them.

All the Prime Ministers within my recollection have been very conscientious in recommending men to the Crown for bishoprics. Asquith even went to the length of reading any books that they had published. And though there may be two or three inferior men on the bench, no one who knows the facts could complain of the present Episcopate as a whole. There is not a very wide choice; that is the fault of the laity, who choose to starve their parish priests. As an American said: "You cannot expect to get all the cardinal virtues for twelve hundred dollars a year."

I cannot think of any alternative system that would work better. In a disestablished Church ambitious men would play for safety, and we should have a set of bishops with, as was unkindly said of one dignitary, a season-ticket on the line of least resistance.

As for entrusting the government of the Church to that talking-shop of bores, the Church Assembly, we remember Clarendon's opinion, that our ecclesiastics "take the worst measure of human affairs of all mankind that can write and read." The lay voice and the democratic principle are palpable camouflage.

The rejection of the new Prayer Book by the House of Commons in 1928 created no indignation in the country, and has now been forgotten. There was never any steam behind it. But a few Churchmen got wildly excited, and spoke of the "interference" of the State.

The real moral of the incident was given by the wise Archbishop of Armagh. "The press in foreign countries was filled with astonishment that a religious issue should so engross the attention of modern people. I confess to a real amazement that this aspect of the subject has not received more attention. It means that, in spite of all appearances to the contrary, the people of Great Britain are profoundly interested in religion."

They are profoundly interested: and as Bishop Burge once said: "If the nation realized all that it owes to the Established Church, it would say, 'In no case will we allow you to be disestablished, not even if you propose it yourself.'"

V

A FUTURE LIFE

I

Is this an improper subject for a secular newspaper?

I do not think so.

If we are not all interested in it, we ought to be,
and from time to time there are popular discussions
which prove that the laity are very much interested
in it.

The clergy seldom speak out, because they are
sincerely perplexed as to what they ought to believe
and to teach about what used to be called the Four
Last Things—Death, Judgment, Heaven, and Hell.

One of the Cambridge Platonists in the seven-
teenth century said, "Heaven is first a temper
and then a place." But unless we are prepared to
forget all that the world has learnt since Copernicus
and Galileo, it can hardly be a place at all. And the
difficulties about time are equally serious. Eternity
cannot be an endless succession of moments, snipped
off at one end but not at the other.

Then there is the moral impossibility of reconciling
the traditional teaching of horrible tortures in
hell with what Christ taught us to believe about
His heavenly Father.

I think the most striking change in religious teaching has been the almost total disappearance of bribes and threats from the pulpit. Most of our teachers have tacitly abandoned hell, and substituted purgatory—a period of remedial discipline for those who will ultimately be saved. This may seem a reasonable thing to believe, but there is no revealed authority for it, nor for any kind of future probation.

These milder views have evoked a protest from Father Godts (*De Paucitate Salvandorum*, 1899), who proved that the unanimous and authoritative teaching of the Church is that by far the greater part of the human race will go to hell.

A writer in the *Universe* for July 20, 1934, declares authoritatively that no Catholic can deny without grievous sin either the reality of the fire in hell, or that those who go there are punished eternally. Father Godts thinks that the laxer doctrine is due to the influence of Protestantism. But Jonathan Edwards is as ferocious as any Catholic; and it was a Scotch Presbyterian woman who in answer to the remonstrance, "I believe you really think that nobody will be saved except yourself and your minister," replied, "I whiles have my doots about the minister."

No, it is not Protestantism, but the spirit of the age, which has made the old teaching about everlasting torment seem intolerable.

But was it ever really believed? One would think

that anyone who was solidly convinced that the large majority of mankind is doomed to endless torture would either go mad, or refrain from having children, or, like John Stuart Mill, would exclaim indignantly, "I will call no Being good who is not what I mean by good when I apply the word to my fellow men; and if there is a Being who can send me to his hell for not so calling him, to hell I will go."

The consciousness of sin has declined so lamentably among us that most people do not think that anybody deserves to be punished severely. *Dieu me pardonnera: c'est son métier.* We think this is a great advance from the harshness of the old doctrine; but there is another side to the question.

There is a great deal about the *fear* of God in the New Testament, and the devil is only shamming to be dead. The dreadful pictures which shock us so much were drawn by good men and women who thought nothing was too bad for them because they were not better men and women. Our contemporaries are good-natured little animals, who want everybody, themselves especially, to have a good time.

Real Christianity is a much sterner creed than this.

The only argument for immortality which our Lord is recorded to have used is His answer to the Sadducees, who denied it: "God is not the God of the dead, but of the living; for all live to Him."

89

This argument is stated very succinctly by St. Augustine, in words which I find very helpful and inspiring. "That which does not perish for God does not perish for itself." The Latin is terser and more impressive: *Quod Deo non perit sibi non perit.*

We too often forget that our belief in human immortality stands or falls with our belief in God. "Because I live, ye shall live also."

In the Fourth Gospel, which is an inspired interpretation of the permanent meaning of the Incarnation, eternal life is independent of time. It is identified with knowledge of God and Christ. In the First Epistle we have the remarkable words: "We know that we have passed from death unto life because we love the brethren"; for God is love, and to know Him is life eternal.

This is the last point which I wish to make. Belief in God is primary; belief in human immortality is secondary and consequential. Any other arguments for survival are worthless.

Some may say: "This spiritual world which you speak of is only a realm of ideals; it has no actual existence."

But we must not separate existence and value in this way. A value which has no existence has no value, and an existence which has no value has no existence. I do not know how to make my meaning plainer than by quoting some words of Dr. Martineau:

"Amid all the sickly talk about ideals, it is well

90

to remember that as long as they are merely a self-painting of the yearning spirit, they have no more solidity than floating air-bubbles, gay in the sunshine and broken by the passing wind. You do not so much as touch the threshold of religion, so long as you are detained by phantoms of your thought; the very gate of entrance to religion, the moment of its new birth, is your discovery that the gleaming ideal is the everlasting real."

A FUTURE LIFE

II

FREDERIC MYERS, who in later life was keenly interested in the evidence for survival, once asked a worthy churchwarden what he really thought would happen to him after death.

The reply was: "I suppose I shall go to everlasting bliss. But I wish you would not talk about such disagreeable subjects."

This is one type of the half-beliefs of which I have written. The churchwarden wished to survive, but preferably as a comfortable church-layman here on earth.

Dr. Schiller and an American friend issued a questionnaire, to which they obtained three thousand answers. Among the questions were: "Would you prefer to live after death or not? Do you desire a future life whatever the conditions might be? Would you be content with a life more or less like your present life? Do you feel the question to be of urgent importance to your mental comfort? Would you like to be certain, or to leave it as a matter of faith?"

Many who answered professed blank indifference.

A clergyman of eighty-five "had no time seriously to consider" the questions.

"From my experience," wrote one man, "ninety-nine out of a hundred say they believe in a future life and act as if there were none."

Some expressed their horror of the idea of annihilation.

One clergyman "would rather be a devil in hell than not be at all."

The poet Tennyson was deeply moved when the subject was mentioned. If he did not believe in a future life, he said, he would put a chloroformed handkerchief over his face and have done with it all.

Meredith was content with an impersonal immortality. "I am the vessel of the thought; the vessel splits, the thought survives."

Lucretius the Epicurean reminds us that there will be no second self to mourn over our extinction. That comfortable creed was summed up in a quatrain—"Nothing to fear in God. Nothing to feel in death. The good—easy to get. The evil—easy to endure."

Very different in tone is the passionate desire for reunion with those whom the writers have loved and lost.

This is evidently by far the strongest motive for believing in a future life. We may be told that it is an obvious reason for wishing for it, but not a reason for believing in it. I do not agree. St. John's words, "We know that we have passed from death unto life because we love the brethren," are no empty words of consolation. Love admits us to the heart of life, as nothing else does. It is the realization in experience of spiritual existence. What it means for personal immortality has been seen by many great thinkers. In all love there must be a subject and an object, and a bond between them which transcends without annulling their separateness. It lifts us above time and space into the life of God Himself. I do not pretend that this guarantees survival in time; it does not. But the source of these hopes, which are often expressed rather crudely, is the conviction that love is stronger than death.

My favourite philosopher, Plotinus, was not a Christian; but this is his vision of eternal life:

"Spirits in heaven see themselves in others. For there all things are transparent, and there is nothing dark or resisting, but everyone is manifest to everyone internally, and all things are manifest, for light is manifest to light. For everyone has all things in himself and sees all things in another, so that all things are everywhere and all is all and each is all, and infinite the glory."

As I have referred to Tennyson, we may recall that Robert Browning rested his belief in immortality on the imperishableness of human love. Unfortunately, this type of belief too easily slides into necromancy, a miserable substitute for the Christian hope. We do not wish to be unfeeling to those who long for some external and tangible evidence that their dear ones are still in existence, but what a starveling hope spiritualism offers! An existence as poor and unsubstantial as that of the Hebrew Sheol or the Greek Hades, and with no guarantee of permanence, even if the power of comforting or frightening the living is supposed to persist for a few years. Such a prospect would add a new terror to death. Would anyone desire it for himself?

We are told that there is scientific evidence for survival. Cases are reported, with much parade of impartiality; but this is emphatically a case where the wish to believe is a reason for doubt. If there are such things as psychic waves in the atmosphere, which may be a vehicle for the communication of thoughts, the discovery would be wholly in favour of materialism. We should see a revival of the notion that spirit is an ultra-gaseous condition of matter, a retrograde theory which obstructed the belief that God is Spirit.

The moment we are asked to accept "scientific evidence" for spiritual truth, the alleged spiritual truth becomes for us neither spiritual nor true.

Dr. Schiller is most impressed by the answers of the mystics, who agree with Spinoza that "we feel and experience that we are immortal."

Some of the answers in this group imply a belief not only in future existence but in past existence. Like many of the ancient Greeks, and Asiatics

95

for thousands of years, these persons believe in reincarnation.

So long as we identify immortality with survival in time, it is easier to believe in it if we assume that we have already lived many lives, and will live many more. But the typical Asiatic does not *want* to live again. He hopes for a dreamless sleep which involves an annihilation of his personality as an individual.

How strangely different from the European view, expressed once for all by Plutarch: "I might almost say that all men and women would readily submit themselves to the teeth of Cerberus and to the punishment of carrying water with a sieve, if they might escape the doom of annihilation."

But Havelock Ellis, writing as an old man, says, "If I am to begin a new life, let me begin it washed clean from all my defects and errors and failures. But the new self would be a self that is not me." I often think the same; I want to be "hatched over again and hatched different." As I am, I am not worth preserving!

Dr. Schiller's last group—the mystics—have the root of the matter in them; but it is not enough to say, "I am sure that I am immortal." We must be ready to give a reason for the faith that is in us.

This I am prepared to do; but I warn my readers that many of them will think that I have given them a stone for bread. The kind of proofs which they would value most are not forthcoming. Spiritual things are spiritually discerned.

Those who wish to go on living because they enjoy their life here, or because they want to be compensated for their bad luck here, or because they have made investments in good works for which they hope, in the words of our hymn, to be "repaid a thousandfold," must go elsewhere for their evidence. Hopes that are pitched too low will not be fulfilled.

A FUTURE LIFE

III

WE may get some help in the difficult and mysterious problem of a future life from the New Testament. St. Paul concludes the finest chapter he ever wrote by reminding us that now we see through a glass darkly—only a blurred reflection of the truth. In another place he says that eye hath not seen nor ear heard, neither hath it entered into the heart of man to conceive the truth about heaven. St. John says, "It doth not yet appear what we shall be." We know next to nothing, because while we live here we could not understand the truth.

And yet the world of eternal and absolute values is or ought to be even more real to us than the world of external facts. Whenever we are in contact with love, or truth, or beauty, we are citizens of that world over which death has no power.

The difficulty is to help ourselves and others to "see the invisible," or, to vary the metaphor, to make a bridge between the two worlds in which we have to live. We try to translate spiritual intuition into concrete fact, and to bridge over the gulf by means of miracles, which are the mysticism of the materialist. We ought to understand that the natural language of devotion is poetry, not science, and that all the higher part of religion is and must be symbolic.

It is a great mistake to interpret the parables of Christ, such as the sheep and the goats, or Dives and Lazarus, as revelations of the future. They are what they profess to be, parables, very much like the "myths" in Plato. That great philosopher realized that the truths of the spiritual world cannot be stated in the language of science, and so he gives them to us in symbolical or mythical form. All his stories about heaven and hell, which have had a great influence upon Christian belief, are meant to be taken in this way. "I do not say that they are true," he says, "but something like them must be near the truth."

My next point is that we are obliged to find room for all our ideas within a framework of time and place, because we are inside that framework ourselves. Philosophers try to escape from this framework, which they see cannot be finally real, by talking of substance and shadow, or appearance and reality. But when we try to think hard on those lines, the old pictures come back. Philosophy, like religion, is incurably poetical and symbolical. It is possible to spiritualize our religion too much; it then becomes nebulous, a luminous haze floating over our real world.

I therefore do not ask my friends to discard their child's picture-books of the next world. Whatever helps us to realize the truth strongly and vividly is right. Only do not let us take these parables for scientific truth. They are on a different plane. If we make this mistake, we shall find reasons for disbelieving not only the symbols, but that which they symbolize.

The traditional symbols are meant to emphasize, in the most vivid and pictorial manner, the infinite importance of a right or wrong moral choice.

In the so-called Ages of Faith, a few sinners were frightened into giving part of their wealth to the Church by way of fire-insurance; but the majority behaved as if there were no future life, either in bliss or torment. How they lived may be gathered from Cotter Morison's *Morality in the Ages of Faith*, or from any candid medieval history. It is quite plain that the whole of traditional eschatology has always belonged to the strange region of half-beliefs, which still occupy a very large space in our minds. The most startling colours were daubed on the picture just because it was only seen through a mist. The times were cruel enough; but this dreadful nightmare was never a part of waking reality, though it provided a hideous justification for religious persecution.

I ask my readers to consider what these half-beliefs, some of which now seem to most of us so unworthy and so repulsive, really mean. It is a too simple solution to cast them aside as barbarous superstitions or priestly impostures. There must have been some respectable foundation for doctrines which lived on for so many centuries. I have tried to suggest what their function is.

I am not at all sure that what I have said will not offend many honest Christians. Some people have an astonishing gift for keeping their minds in watertight compartments. The religious compartment may contain beliefs of almost unbelievable crudity. Let me give three examples which I happen to have heard of.

When the *Titanic* was going down, an American millionaire retired to his cabin, not to say his prayers but to dress for dinner. He explained that he wished to go before his Maker looking like a gentleman.

An old admiral employed a Jewish Rabbi to teach him Hebrew. His clergyman asked him why he wished to spend his old age in this peculiar manner. He replied: "I know that my life has not been all that it should be; but I hope to obtain mercy and to be admitted to Abraham's bosom. And I should like to be able to talk to Abraham in his own language."

An equally distinguished army officer took me to task for saying in one of my books that life must be a very rare phenomenon in the universe, because it can only exist within rather narrow limits of temperature. My friend objected that life can certainly exist in hell, though the temperature there is terrific.

My point is that these three men had all risen

to the top of their professions. They were not at all men who could be laughed at; and yet how infantile were their mental processes on one side!

The clergyman is often confronted with this extreme simplicity, in quarters where he would not have expected to find it; and on the other side with vulgar, self-satisfied rationalism, which dismisses the belief in eternal life, no matter what form it may take, as absurd nonsense.

VI

ARE CHRISTIANS NARROW-MINDED?

In John Bailey's delightful *Letters and Diaries* there is a question which set me thinking.

The writer, an earnest Christian as well as a brilliant humorist, asks himself whether St. Paul was right in speaking of the depth and height and *breadth* of the Gospel. Christianity enriches life by giving it height and depth—that is certain. But does it broaden the mind, or does it often seem to have the opposite effect?

If we want a broad view of any great problem should we go to a Churchman to ask for it?

A rather awkward question for an ecclesiastic! But it is one which we ought not to shirk. For even if our heads are in the clouds, our feet must remain planted on the earth, and we do not want to resemble the philosopher Thales, who tumbled into a well while he was meditating on ultimate reality and the supreme good.

We are bidden to walk on the narrow way, but we need not walk in blinkers. There are religions of authority and there are religions of the Spirit. Those who, as a matter of principle, submit themselves to authority keep their minds tight shut. They will not consider the possibility that Holy Church may be wrong. In consequence, when any modern controversial question is raised—for example, birth-control or euthanasia or divorce—it is useless to expect anything helpful from them.

They may often be right—authority often expresses the mature wisdom and experience of the race—but since they refuse to treat as open questions matters on which authority has given a decision, they can neither learn anything nor teach us anything. They often profess to argue candidly, but we know in advance what the conclusion will be. They do not admit either the right or the duty of private judgment.

Bigotry and sectarianism have dogged the footsteps of Christianity from the very first. To this day there is no abatement in the narrow intolerance of the great Church of authority, and there are some Protestant societies where narrow-mindedness, though less aggressive, is more absurd. Sectarianism always generates a crop of taboos—harmless things that must not be done, such as eating a mutton-chop on Friday, or the use of alcohol or tobacco.

The Psalmist contemplating these petty prohibitions could hardly have said, "Thy commandment is exceeding broad."

But is this an indictment against Christianity, or only against Christians? In our Lord's time the people with shut minds did not follow Christ; they crucified Him; and they would make things very unpleasant for Him if He came back to earth. It is always the sons of the men who killed the prophets who build their sepulchres.

Religion begins as an illumination; but it is soon half strangled by the institutions which were formed to protect it. The prophet is followed by the "adherent"; the word is well chosen.

There is, however, another thing which we must bear in mind. The saint is a specialist, and the specialist always has to pay a price for concentrating on one subject. As Christ warned us, he who would win the pearl of great price must be prepared to sell all that he has to obtain it.

In earlier times, saintship was a recognized career, and the monks and mystics were willing to sacrifice all that other men desire in the hope of being rewarded with the beatific vision. Rightly or wrongly, we do not think that this degree of renunciation is required of us, and we do not consider that the life of the extreme ascetic is wholesome or desirable. We were not sent into the world to run away from it. But everyone who sets before him one supreme object in life must renounce a great deal. We cannot excel in anything without giving up several other things which we might be and do and learn.

We must all specialize, if we would do anything worth doing. But the higher the object of our quest the less we shall be narrowed by it. The time-honoured classification of the absolute values—the things that are worth pursuing for their own sake,

and not as instruments for getting something else
—as the Good, the True and the Beautiful, will
do well enough for us. The religious man, the
scholar or scientist, and the artist or poet, are
engaged in one or other of these three quests. They
are not entirely separate from each other; the three
paths up the hill of the Lord meet at the top; but
most men have to concentrate on one of the three,
and all are legitimate.

My point is that these absolute values all have
a universal quality, and that even the specialist in
any one of them is not seriously narrowed by his
concentration. The best Christians that I have
known have not been narrow-minded—men, for
example, like Archbishop Davidson, whose *Life* is
now being much discussed. But wherever we find
bigotry and sectarianism, wherever a man aims
at being not a good Christian but a good Catholic
or a good Churchman, narrowness appears at once,
and in its worst form, because it shows itself in
arrogance, unscrupulous proselytism and fierce
uncharitableness.

Religion, as Professor Whitehead has said, is not
always a good thing; it may be a very bad thing
not only for its possessor but for society. It has held
back civilization and progress again and again.
But this is because the best is the most easily
corrupted.

Sane Christianity is broad as well as high and
deep; but we seldom give it a trial.

VII

RELIGION AND CONDUCT

WHEN we think of having business dealings with a man of whom we know little, what precautions do we usually take? We ask one or two friends to testify to his integrity. We make his acquaintance, and judge by the expression of his face, by his conversation, by what we can learn about the general set of his actions, and his reputation, whether he is a man to be trusted.

One question we seldom ask what church, if any, does he attend, and what, if any, are his religious beliefs? We do not think that this information would help us much. Are we to infer that in our heart of hearts we know that a man's religion is no clue to his character?

In the first place, it is not true that we never make such inquiries. In matters of business we have to beware of the man who keeps his conscience in watertight compartments, like Mr. Bulstrode in George Eliot's masterpiece, *Middlemarch*, to whom it had never occurred that strict honesty in money affairs had anything to do with what he called the scheme of salvation. This type exists, but is less common than it was a hundred years ago.

We have also to remember that each profession has its own standard of morality. A solicitor or merchant, unless he is a rogue, may be a pleasanter man to do business with than a clergyman, who is sometimes difficult, partly from ignorance and partly because scrupulous fairness in business is not for him the primary virtue.

There is also an emotional type of men and women, given to what Dean Page Roberts used to call "devotionality," who are not always to be trusted in matters of everyday morality.

Lastly, there is the fanatical Churchman, who in serving the interests of his Church thinks that the end justifies the means, and is far more unscrupulous than the ordinary man of the world.

But in other relations of life we do not consider religion unimportant.

When a man (or woman) is contemplating marriage, he wants above all things to feel himself secure against what I believe are called in business "third party risks," and here it makes all the difference whether a possible partner is a sincere Christian or not.

And surely there are other Christian virtues, such as readiness to forgive injuries, kindness and generosity, which are so far recognized factors in the Christian character that no one who takes his religion seriously can entirely disregard them.

The snare is that there is often a great difference between what we say we believe, what we think we believe, and what we really believe.

Do we know what we really believe? We are never free from the danger of self-deception. We cannot live in the world without to some extent acting the part which we wish to exhibit. And yet Christ condemned this acting so strongly that the Greek word for actor, "hypocrite," has had a bad meaning ever since.

The great thing, I suppose, is to have nothing to conceal—to make our lives all of a piece.

When I was ordained, the Bishop (Dr. King, of Lincoln) said to me: "Be disinterested. That is the only thing that matters." I have never forgotten this advice, which goes to the root of the matter. If disinterestedness is the heart of religion, it would be absurd to say that religion makes no difference to a man's conduct and character.

But I am not preaching a sermon. I want to raise this question: Now that most of our people, especially in the working class, "go nowhere," and neglect all the ordinances of religion, do we find any deterioration in the national character? To begin with, is the average non-churchgoer really irreligious?

Anti-religious, in this country, he is not. There is very little of the hatred of religion which is so common on the Continent.

Christianity, with its warning "Take heed and beware of covetousness," stands aloof from political quarrels. It is revolutionary, but not in a political sense. It has its own standard of values, among which money and the things which money will buy hold a very subordinate place.

The typical Englishman, who is not a Communist, would probably say that he believes in God, though he does not often think of Him, and he has a very sincere admiration for the character of Jesus Christ. He believes in kindness, and practises it. He dislikes hypocrisy, hard-heartedness and calculating worldliness, the three things which Christ also most condemned. We can fancy our Master saying to such a one, "Thou art not far from the Kingdom of God."

Were people morally any better when gaudy promises and lurid threats resounded from the pulpit, and when the priest was the keeper of the individual conscience? I do not think they were. Nevertheless, two things must be said on the other side.

It was not a secularized and prosaic Christianity which converted Europe. In the medieval Church, in the midst of cruelty, ignorance and superstition, there was a class of "religious" men and women who exhibited the beauty of holiness and "heroic" spirituality in a way which is hardly to be found in our modern society. We ought to have a few shining examples of a much higher standard than the majority can hope to reach.

The other question is this. Most of our morality is traditional. The agnostics of the last century for the most part accepted the Christian standard of conduct as a matter of course. They lived strict lives themselves, and blamed those who acted otherwise.

But Christian ethics are based on the Christian revelation and the authority of the Church, in which these agnostics did not believe. Since the war, all authority has been very much relaxed, and everyone is asking, "Why shouldn't I?" We are loose from our moorings, and there is really no accepted standard of right and wrong. In so far as Christian conduct is merely traditional, we must expect to see it gradually discarded.

But I do not think we are getting worse. Our religion has struck very deep roots into the national life. As the Latin proverb says, "You may drive out human nature with a pitchfork; she will always come back." She will come back with her imperfections, but with her nobleness too.

VIII

THE OLD TESTAMENT

From time to time we hear complaints that our religion, as represented in our Church services, is too Jewish. There is as much of the Old Testament as of the New in our forms of worship.

It is true that we no longer publicly read the Pentateuch straight through, chapter by chapter, including some chapters of Genesis which are by no means suited to the young person, being rather like some of the less edifying stories in the *Arabian Nights*. But in our Anglican marriage-service we pertinaciously hold up the example of the polygamous patriarchs as a model for our young couples; and some of the Psalms, which are long-drawn Oriental curses, are still ordered to be sung, though they are no longer often heard, since the rejection of the New Prayer Book by the House of Commons has been followed by a system of go-as-you-please, every vicar doing what is right in his own eyes.

I remember the debate in Convocation about the cursing psalms. One worthy dean pleaded for their retention because they expressed our justifiable feelings towards the Germans. (It was during the war.) An excellent archdeacon regretted the result of the voting, which gave a majority in favour of the change. I said, "But don't you think some of them are rather strong—for instance, the verse about throwing Babylonian children against the stones?" "I thought," he said severely, "that every educated Christian knew that those verses apply exclusively to our spiritual enemies."

There are also some verses in the Psalms which are quite unintelligible to the average worshipper.

I should be in favour of a more drastic revision than the book which Parliament refused to ratify. The Old Testament is only one of the streams which flowed together to make Europe Christian. For, after all, we are Europeans; Christianity is the least Asiatic of all the great religions. When St. Paul won Europe for Christ, he lost Asia.

And yet it would be a fatal mistake to discard the Old Testament altogether. Judaism is the religion of faith and hope. "Shall not the Judge of all the earth do right?" That is the leading motive of the Old Testament. Every possible answer is discussed, inconclusively; but that much-tried nation has never lost hope, and in consequence the Jews have stood by the graves of all their oppressors in turn.

Besides, what incomparable beauties there are in the Hebrew Scriptures, for those who can appreciate them! Such Psalms as those numbered 15, 18, 34, 50, 51, 73, 90, 91, 103, and several others, are priceless; and for patriotic poetry it would be hard to beat the song of Deborah and the description of the defeat of the Assyrians.

Even in Genesis there are passages which without undue ingenuity may be made to yield beautiful allegories of human life as we all know it. Take, for instance, that very Oriental "supplanter" Jacob. We have heard the story of the sporting parson who, after reading a conventional borrowed sermon about Esau and Jacob, shut his book with a snap and extemporized for the first time in his life. "And so, my brethren, you see that in this nefarious transaction Esau behaved like a gentleman and a sportsman, and Jacob like a dirty little Jew as he was!" This, no doubt, woke up his congregation.

But look at the story of Jacob's two visions. The first, as he lay among the rugged boulders of Bethel, was a dream of a ladder from earth to heaven, a double stairway, with the messengers of God hurrying up and down. Shall we call these messengers prayers and blessings? Or shall we think of all the prophets and wise men, philosophers and poets, saints and heroes, who have searched and thought and prayed and fasted and killed and died, to get a foot on that ladder reaching from earth to heaven? They have asked, "Why did we ever come down, and how can we get back?"

But the young man's dream on the hard stones is a happy one. Life is before him, and the whole world is God's house.

114

Very different is the second vision, which is unlike anything else in the Old Testament.

Jacob is about to cross the brook Jabbok, to meet the brother whom he has wronged. (I know what the commentators say about the origin of the story, and it does not matter to us here.) It is a weird dream of a wrestling-match in the dark all through the night with an unknown adversary, who will neither conquer nor yield, who refuses to give his name, but at last consents to give his blessing. Jacob is left alone as the morning breaks, limping but victorious. He called the scene of his first dream Bethel, the House of God; the scene of the second he called Peniel, the Face of God, that face which no man can see and live.

As we advance in years, and look back over our past life, does it not seem to us that we have been wrestling all the time in the dark and that we do not know who our opponent has been—God or devil, or more probably neither, but just the other half of ourselves? But perhaps when we are growing old, and the struggle becomes less severe—for, although there is no exemption from Christ's army at fifty, at seventy we do begin to take off our armour and think of rest—perhaps when we are growing old we feel that our unseen companion is not an enemy at all, but a friend, and the greatest of all friends.

Then we would fain know for certain who and what He is. We say, "Tell me Thy name," and we are not told. But, since we have striven all the night, with many painful falls probably, we say, "I will not let Thee go unless Thou bless me." And this request, we may hope, is not refused. There are streaks of dawn in the sky. Heaven's morning breaks and earth's vain shadows flee. The end of life's dream is approaching, and when we awake perhaps we shall know why "the name of that place is called Peniel."

Have I been reading too much into a bit of primitive folk-lore? Ought we to read the Bible "like any other book"? Not entirely, I think; and, besides, the value of a book to us is what we can find in it.

Whether we are reading the Bible, or any other great book, the best part of our reading is when we put the volume down and think about it. If it is a devotional book the thinking may well be on our knees.

IX

THE FIRST CHRISTIAN MYSTIC

A WELL-WRITTEN book on *The Mind of St. Paul*, by Irwin Edman (Jonathan Cape), may be an excuse for summing up the results of recent scholarship on the personality of the Apostle to the Gentiles.

We know more about St. Paul than about any other character of antiquity except Marcus Tullius Cicero, though we shall never know for certain whether he was executed after his two years' imprisonment at Rome, or whether he was liberated when his accusers at Jerusalem failed to appear. Personally, I find it difficult to believe that St. Luke, a skilled man of letters, would have ended his book so tamely, if he might have described the martyrdom of his hero.

But St. Paul's letters are a human document of the first importance. They are real letters, written hastily; but they have become canonical scriptures, and their author has been buried under a mountain of dry systematic theology. Paul has been lost in Paulinism.

In reality he was not a learned theologian. It is not quite certain that he read any books except the Old Testament in Greek. He was, as Mr. Edman says, a Jewish rabbi in his method, a Greek mystic in feeling and temper.

German professors have written about him as if he was even such a one as themselves. But he was a travelling missionary, like George Fox or John Wesley, though intellectually far above either of them.

The key to the amazing and enduring success of his work, which may be compared with the conquests of Alexander the Great, though in the reverse direction, is to be found in his origin. He was a Jew, but a Jew of the Dispersion, who wrote and thought in Greek, and he was a Roman citizen.

The partially assimilated Jew is a familiar figure all over the world, and Tarsus, St. Paul's birthplace, was not only a trade centre, but a university town. He wrote and thought in Greek, but he retained important beliefs which were Jewish, not Greek, and this combination, which leaves many ragged edges, has been the faith of the civilized world for nearly two thousand years.

Some such fusion of eastern and western thought might have taken place without St. Paul; but we should hardly be wrong if we credited him with the greatest achievement in human history.

The Jewish factors in his creed were his belief in one God—he never put Christ quite on an equality with the Father; his Oriental prejudice against the symbolic worship of images; his firm conviction of the "righteousness" of God; and the importance which he gives to history, whether past or future.

His belief in the approaching end of the age and in the return of Christ to earth was evidently fading in his later epistles; but he never consciously abandoned it, though Messianism meant very little outside Palestine. Ever since St. Paul, the Church has wavered between the late-Jewish belief in the resurrection of the body, and the Greek (Orphic) belief in the immortality of the soul, or rather it has tried, not very successfully, to combine them.

The Greek element in his faith had, of course, nothing to do with the official cult of the Olympian gods. It belonged rather to the mystery religions which pervaded the Mediterranean world.

These were confraternities which participated in sacred rites, usually guarded by vows of secrecy. Their chief characteristics were ceremonies of purification, which by some were interpreted magically; the promise of spiritual communion with some deity, often a dying and rising saviour, whose life is sacramentally imparted to his worshippers; and thirdly, the hope of immortality, which is assured to those who are initiated. We need not suppose that St. Paul was ever attracted by these pagan societies; it is certain that he was not. But, nevertheless, it was as a mystery religion that Europe accepted Christianity; mystery is the Greek word which the Latins rendered, poorly enough, by their word sacrament. All this very essential part of St. Paul's Gospel had nothing to do with Palestinian Judaism. The later epistles are full of the technical terms of the mysteries, which a Greek writer, in sympathy with this type of religion, could hardly avoid.

The apostle regarded his conversion as sudden and miraculous. He was convinced that he had "seen" the glorified Christ; and this revelation animated the whole of his subsequent life.

Attempts to explain this vision as a merely psychological or pathological seizure—perhaps a kind of sunstroke—are unsatisfactory, since the effects were out of all proportion to the alleged cause. Whether he was subconsciously influenced by having witnessed the heroic death of Stephen, we cannot say. What is certain is first, that the Christianity which he persecuted was not the Messianic Judaism of the Twelve, with whom he never interfered, but the Liberal Christianity of Stephen and other Hellenists; and second, that it was this Christianity, the faith of Stephen not that of James the Lord's brother, to which he was suddenly converted.

St. Paul is the first and greatest of the Christian mystics. I do not lay stress so much on the "visions and revelations" to which he was subject, though they are sufficient to prove that he had the mystical temperament.

What is decisive is his strong conviction that his own personality was submerged in Christ. "I live, yet not I, but Christ liveth in me." It was not the suffering and dying Jesus but the risen and deathless Christ with whom he was united.

The passion, death and resurrection of Christ were historical facts, certainly; but their permanent value was sacramental, almost dramatic. They revealed the normal process of redemption, the death to sin and the new birth to righteousness, the path which we all have to tread. We must not whittle away the very plain language in which this is expressed.

That this very human though very heroic saint has escaped the dubious honour of being coaxed and wheedled by Catholic piety is perhaps not surprising. We know too much about him.

But why is he actively disliked? The German scholar Lagarde abuses him like a personal enemy. Nietzsche calls him "one of the most ambitious of men, an exceedingly unpleasant person both to himself and others."

I suppose the chief gravamen against him is that he takes the conflict between flesh and spirit very seriously. Modern Freudians do not like to be told to crucify the flesh with the affections and lusts, and they do not understand why St. Paul is so stern about impurity.

Well, a modern missionary at Port Said or Singapore might speak severely on this subject, and Corinth was worse than either. His argument is that the body must not be soiled because it is the shrine of the Holy Spirit. To say that St. Paul was a harsh ascetic is simply not true.

X

THE JUDGMENT OF PARIS

PARIS, the son of Priam and Hecuba, King and Queen of Troy, was kidnapped as a child and brought up in a shepherd's family. When he was a young man, Zeus, the father of gods and men, appointed him as judge in a dispute between Hera (Juno), Athene (Minerva) and Aphrodite (Venus) as to which of them was the most beautiful.

Lucian, Rubens and Tennyson agree that the three goddesses appeared before Paris "disrobed." In the picture by Rubens, a rustic is leering at three fat Dutchwomen, who would have been wiser not to remove their gowns.

But I do not believe it. The Greeks in their golden age represented their gods stark naked; but as far as I remember (I hope I am not wrong) there is no statue of a naked goddess till a later period of Hellenic art. Besides, what would a goddess be without her attributes? The clothes are the man, and the woman, as Carlyle showed in *Sartor Resartus*.

No; Hera wore a crown like a battlemented tower. Athene had a helmet, a shield and a spear. Aphrodite had at least her magic girdle, and probably a semi-transparent robe.

Of course they all offered bribes; were they not in the Levant? Hera offered him Power; in Tennyson's words, "Proffer of royal power, ample rule, unquestioned, overflowing revenue, honour and homage—power which in all action is the end of all, power fitted to the season, wisdom-bred and throned of wisdom—from all neighbour-crowns alliance and allegiance." Paris, according to Lucian, not being at all ambitious, takes a virtuous line and says he is not to be bribed.

Next comes Athene, who in Lucian's story promises him victory in war. Paris replies that he is a pacifist by conviction. But Athene had better things than this to offer, as Tennyson shows:

"Self-reverence, self-knowledge, self-control, these three alone lead life to sovereign power. Yet not for power (power of herself would come uncalled for) but to live by law, acting the law we live by without fear; and, because right is right, to follow right were wisdom in the scorn of consequence."

The gifts of Athene are all the gifts of the disciplined intellect—what the Greeks called philosophy, the love of wisdom. These our religion calls the Seven Gifts of the Holy Spirit—wisdom and understanding, counsel and might, knowledge, the fear of the Lord, and quick understanding in the fear of the Lord. The Councils of the Church opened with a prayer to the Holy Spirit for intellectual inspiration.

Paris did not find this offer attractive. In the pastures of Ida, philosophy is not studied; and he was a young man.

The third goddess offered him, without any preamble, "the fairest and most loving wife in Greece," Helen, who, unfortunately, was already married to Menelaus of Sparta. So Paris gave the apple to Aphrodite, and with her help carried off Helen. The Trojan War was the consequence.

But that is not the end of the story. Did Paris get Helen after all? It seems not. The poet Stesichorus wrote a poem in which he implied that Helen was no better than she should be. For this criticism of Aphrodite, he was stricken with blindness, and only recovered his sight when he had written a retractation, in which he said, not that love justifies any breaches of morality (these poor benighted heathens did not live in the twentieth century) but that Helen never went to Troy at all. She was spirited away to Egypt, and Paris clasped no real woman but a phantom.

And sure enough, when Telemachus, the son of Odysseus, visits Sparta, he finds Menelaus and Helen living together as if nothing had happened, and Helen, the perfect hostess, gives "the dear child" a piece of embroidery, worked by her own hands. But "the gods gave Helen no more children, after she bore the lovely Hermione."

These old stories are frequently half-conscious allegories. How often do the three goddesses present themselves to a young man and invite him to choose between them! Worldly ambition, the cultivation of mind and character, sensual gratification—which shall he choose?

Christianity names three spiritual enemies—the World, that is Hera; the Flesh, that is Aphrodite; but Athene is certainly not the Devil. Athene rather represents the humanist ideal, which had partly faded from view in the days of the early Church. But the rivalry between the World and the Flesh determines the course of more lives.

Occasionally the battle is fought out on a conspicuous stage. Shakespeare's *Antony and Cleopatra* is one of the finest tragedies ever written, because the sufferer is no base criminal, but the victim of what Aristotle, in his discussion of tragedy, calls a great mistake.

Antony's officers can see nothing in his infatuation for Cleopatra but a degrading passion. "His captain's heart, which in the scuffles of great fights hath burst the buckles on his breast, reneges all temper, and is become the bellows and the fan to cool a gipsy's lust."

But Shakespeare will not allow us to despise Antony. Infatuated he was; he thought the world well lost for love; but what a tremendous sacrifice he made! The greatest prize in the world—to be emperor of the vast dominions which then, as was thought, comprised the whole civilized world, that was the stake. The romantic will always shed tears over Antony and Cleopatra, as over Paolo and Francesca in Dante.

And yet it will not do. The sanctity of marriage is no invention of the Christian Church, still less of Victorian prudery. It is a tragedy indeed when Sir Lancelot allows himself to be so far entangled with Guinevere that, "his honour rooted in dishonour stood, and faith unfaithful kept him falsely true." But let anyone read the closing scenes in the lives of the two lovers in Sir Thomas Malory, one of the most exquisite things in English literature. They are forgiven, yes: but after what repentance and surrender of all to God. And what misery their sin had caused—the ruin of King Arthur's life's work.

PSYCHOLOGY

I

OPTIMISM AND PESSIMISM

LET us imagine an altercation between a Pessimist and an Optimist.

P.—You are the kind of person who would buy from a Jew and sell to a Scot and expect to make a profit.

O.—You are the kind of person who sold out your perfectly sound Australian stocks in a panic for half their value.

P.—You are always saying that there is a good time coming; and it never comes.

O.—You are always saying that the country is going to the dogs; and it never gets there.

P.—"Send me hence ten thousand miles from a face that always smiles."

O.—I can't think why it is that all the Christians I meet look so melancholy.

P.—The sight of you, sir, would make any Christian melancholy.

O.—Go along with you, and of two evils choose both.

At this point a bystander might intervene. "One of you is a barometer stuck at set fair; the other is a barometer stuck at stormy; I would not give sixpence for either of you."

The truth is that we often do not know whether

our neighbours are happy or unhappy. "The heart knoweth its own bitterness, and a stranger doth not intermeddle with its joy." One of the most woebegone faces that I have known belonged to a brilliant wit, who, I believe, was really a happy man. The laughing philosopher often pretends to be jolly just to show that fate cannot touch him; that was the boast of all the ancient philosophers.

"Master," said a scholar of Balliol to Jowett, *à propos* of the Stoic and Epicurean paradoxes, "do you really think a good man could be happy on the rack?" The master, after a pause, replied, "Well, perhaps a very good man on a *very* bad rack."

As for the pessimist, he is a man who likes to be agreeably surprised when things turn out better than he had chosen to expect. "Blessed is he who expects nothing, for he shall never be disappointed."

But do we always know the truth about our own feelings? Perhaps we are never so happy or unhappy as we think we are. Superficially, I think the happiest people are the vain, who are entirely satisfied to be themselves; and they are very irritating to their neighbours. The proud, on the other hand, are almost always unhappy. But what are we to say about the confessions which some great and successful men have made about themselves?

The German statesman, von Bülow, returning to Berlin when Bismarck was at the zenith of his fame and success, found him extremely depressed. Bülow suggested to his chief that if anyone was entitled to feel himself a happy man, it was he. Bismarck replied that he could not honestly remember having been happy for more than three days in all his life, which had been one unceasing struggle. He had been constantly assailed by envy, hatred and malice, and thwarted by the folly and imbecility of his colleagues and subordinates.

No doubt it was so, and Bismarck was a pretty good hater himself; but can we doubt that he enjoyed the game when he was not in low spirits?

Nevertheless, I agree with Borrow, in a well-known though rather too rhetorical passage of *Lavengro*, that the optimists never do anything great in the world. Why should they want to change anything in the best of all possible worlds? ("This is the best of all possible worlds," said the philosopher Bradley, "and everything in it is a necessary evil.") "Thou wouldst be joyous, wouldst thou? Then be a fool. Who have been the wise ones, the mighty ones, the conquering ones of the earth? The joyous? I believe it not."

Of course we may answer that the pessimist is equally ineffective. The typical pessimist in literature is Schopenhauer, who tells us that we alternate between discontent and boredom. All the objects of human desire are just baits by which Nature seeks to get her hook in our nose, and makes us serve her purposes, which are not our own. "Then make them your own," a Stoic would reply, "make them your own, and be happy."

The man who is always afraid of being duped will not make much of his life, and if the nature of things is in a conspiracy to deceive us, what escape can there be except by renouncing life itself? But there is no reason to believe anything of the kind.

As regards our private affairs and our own characters, I think pessimism is to be fought against. For myself I have had many troubles; most of them never happened. The best moralists, from St. Paul to Spinoza, have warned us against despondency, which the medieval casuists called by the name of Acedia, and classed among the seven deadly sins. We blame our nerves or livers; but we ought never to incur the censure which St. Paul lays upon the pagan society of his day—"having no hope, and without God in the world." The Jews, on the contrary, "against hope believed in hope"; their hopefulness was justified. There are no more Assyrians or Babylonians or Persians or Greeks or Romans; but the Jews, in spite of Hitler, are always with us, and generally on the top.

One of my favourite mottoes is this from Blake:

> Joy and woe are woven fine,
> A clothing for the soul divine.
> Under every grief and pine
> Runs a joy with silken twine.
> It is right it should be so;
> Man was made for joy and woe;
> And when this we rightly know
> Safely through the world we go.

But about public affairs, can we be reasonably hopeful? Of course we may agree with Dr. Johnson, who, when Boswell said, "If I were in Parliament I should be vexed if things went wrong," replied, "That's cant, sir. Public affairs vex no man."

I suppose they did not, in that comfortable eighteenth century; but they do vex us, and rightly. A contemporary of Johnson, the Comte de Guibert, wrote in 1770: "To-day the whole of Europe is civilized. Wars have become less cruel. Save in combat no blood is shed; prisoners are respected; towns are no more destroyed; the countryside is no more ravaged; conquered peoples are only obliged to pay some sort of contributions, which are often less than the taxes they paid to their own sovereign."

Well, after reading that, it is not easy to leave off on a note of optimism. But there is a proverb that the darkest hour comes before the dawn, and another that "things refuse to be badly administered for long."

133

II

SOLITUDE

MATTHEW ARNOLD, writing before the days of
motor-cars, complains that his countrymen are
always hurrying and rushing about, so that "we
never once possess our souls before we die." We
are accustomed to think of our souls as our most
precious possession. To lose our souls is final and
complete failure. And yet most people spend their
lives in running away from themselves. The soul is
a gentleman whose acquaintance they have no
desire to make. If they are condemned to his
society for more than a few minutes, they find him
such an intolerable bore that they long to meet
a friend, or even an enemy. They take their
holidays in crowds, though nothing is more detestable than a crowd.

Forty miles an hour on the roads is not fast
enough to get away from the objectionable fellow.
Perhaps if we go to a foreign country he will not
find us. Meanwhile we can always chatter, or read,
or listen, or watch something going on.

To the Oriental all this is quite incomprehensible.
For him meditation is the noblest activity, and
"saintship is the ceasing from all works." A great
many Europeans have thought as he does. "Oh,
Solitude, sole happiness!" exclaims St. Bernard.

"The nurse of full-grown souls is solitude," says Lowell. "A talent grows in solitude, a character in the stream of the world," is Goethe's wise judgment. "When from our better selves we have too long been parted by the hurrying world, and droop, sick of its business, of its pleasures tired, how gracious, how benign is solitude!" so Wordsworth writes, though later he confesses, "I was taught to feel perhaps too much the self-sufficing power of solitude."

Poets and philosophers are not the best witnesses, because the poet lavishes on the objects of his imagination the attentions which common men pay to their neighbours.

There are some people, I know, who fancy that they are attracted by nature, or by God, when they are really only repelled by man. But the real poet and philosopher has substituted the society of ideas for that of things and persons; his mind to him a kingdom is. He is lonely not so much by choice as because he seldom finds anyone to share his thoughts. And when the mystic assures us that the Divine presence in his soul is the best society, we must not presume to dispute the truth of his experience.

But does this justify the vast organizations which for many centuries covered Europe, Asia and North Africa with monasteries, convents and hermitages, the object of which was to enable men and women to withdraw from the society of their fellow men, and to live during the greater part of every day in silent meditation?

The rule of silence and solitude was more severe in some institutions than in others. The Trappists are even now pledged to almost unbroken silence: and the hermits sometimes lived almost like wild beasts. The hermits have left very few successors; but to this day there are thousands of men and tens of thousands of women who have deliberately chosen the conventual life; and as far as the outside world is permitted to know, very few of them wish to leave it.

It is always a good rule, says Lippmann, to discard any idea based on the premise that the best minds of another age were congenitally inferior to our own. We must try to understand the attraction of a mode of living which most of our contemporaries would find intolerable.

We may suspect that a great many women have taken refuge in the cloister because Cupid has left them alone, and a great many men because Cupid will not leave them alone. Nor is Cupid the only enemy of peace. "The whole world lieth in the Evil One," says St. John. Greed, injustice and cruelty have made life in the world so unpleasant that the opportunity to escape from it altogether seems to many very attractive.

The rule of silence cannot be very onerous, for what is there to talk about in a monastery? Meditation, difficult at first, may become delightful;

and we must not forget that every year spent in a monastery or convent makes its inmates more unfit to live anywhere else. They would be like snails without their shells.

Solitude and celibacy seem at first sight to simplify the problems of life enormously. In the Dark Ages the temptation to run away from society was much greater than it is now. Nothing is more absurd than to try to whitewash that dreadful period. Read, for example, Luchaire's book on France in the reign of Philippe Auguste. There was no treason in despairing of society instead of living in the world and trying to make it better; for nobody then believed that humanity had a long future before it. "The world is very evil, the times are waxing late," was the universal belief.

These communities of mostly silent and solitary men and women are hitherto the only successful experiments in communism. Modern communism offers some of the same attractions, especially freedom from anxiety. The community, or the State, exacts poverty and obedience, and guarantees a maintenance, however simple.

In some of the monasteries with milder discipline there was, no doubt, plenty of sociability. Human nature asserted itself against all the old strict rules. And on the other side there are many solitary people among us who do not live the "religious" life.

Some people are merely shy, and suffer tortures

of isolation. They can console themselves for being where they are only by thinking of the inconceivable number of places where they are not. But they hate their loneliness, and there is no kinder act of Christian charity than to draw them out of their shells and cure them of what modern psychologists call their inferiority complex.

An eminent philosopher has recently said that a man's religion is what he does with his solitariness. This may easily be misunderstood; but if he means that the soul is dyed the colour of its leisure thoughts, and that "as a man thinketh in his heart so is he," it is true.

Nothing isolates a man from his fellows so much as the unamiable sin of pride, which Christianity, the religion of love, has always treated very seriously. We laugh at the vain man and like him; we sometimes admire the proud man, but we cannot like him, and, indeed, we ought to pity him.

On the whole, though we should follow George Herbert's advice, "By all means use some times to be alone," I think that solitude is the death of all but the strongest virtue.

Few people now read Abraham Cowley; but there is a passage of his which I can never forget. It tells the truth with deadly emphasis. "The truth of the matter is that solitude can be well fitted but upon a very few persons. If the mind be possest with any lust or passion, a man had better be in a fair than in a wood alone. The passions may, like petty thieves, cheat us, perhaps, and pick our pockets in the midst of company; but, like robbers, they use to strip and bind and murder us when they catch us alone. This is but to retreat from man and to fall into the hands of devils. It is like the punishment of parricides among the Romans, to be sewed into a bag with an ape, a dog, and a serpent."

III

TWO TYPES OF MIND

DURING the war the Americans subjected between
one and two millions of their recruits to a simple
examination in general intelligence, the object
being to sort out those who were fit for military
duties in which brains were desirable. The result
was so humiliating for admirers of democracy that
the tests, which were sensible and honestly applied,
were received with great indignation.

The average adult male citizen of the great
republic is, it appears, mentally a little boy at a
preparatory school, between eleven and thirteen
years old. The shock would have been less if it
had been realized that the human brain is normally
at its best at the age of about sixteen. As we grow
older we gain experience and knowledge and caution;
but in sheer innate cleverness we do not, so they
tell us, make much further progress after fifteen.

I may add that the American experiment brought
out those whose families came from north-western
Europe at the top of the list. This rather shakes
my confidence in the examination, for though
we may be morally superior to foreigners (I think
we are!) I should not have said that the average
Briton is quick-witted or intelligent, as compared
with the Italian or the Jew.

Perhaps the most useful classification of intelligence is that of the psychologist Jung, who divides mankind into "extraverts" and "introverts." (I found the latter word, to my surprise, in a book a hundred years old.) They are not pretty words, but they hardly need explanation.

The extravert lives in his environment. For him the outside world is real; all that interests him comes to him from without. He is bored and unhappy when he is alone; his inner life is so poor and empty that he instinctively seeks a crowd, and prefers the most vapid conversation to silence.

The introvert is the man whose mind to him a kingdom is. He is unobservant and "absent-minded," as other people say, though his mind is really the only thing that is not absent. The outside world is as hazy to him as the inner world is to the opposite type. He is a natural mystic.

The two types cannot understand each other and are always fighting. Unfortunately they despise and dislike each other. The practical man who gets things done thinks the dreamer a poor creature. The introvert has no respect for the busybody who surrounds himself with the symbols of achievements which seem to him worthless.

Your practical man, he says, knows the price of everything and the value of nothing. Our needs are really very simple. Why complicate life and make the art of living, which is an easy thing, unnecessarily difficult?

This quarrel breaks out in almost all human
interests. In philosophy there are some who resent
change and movement; they say, in the words of
the hymn, "O Thou, who changest not, abide
with me." They argue that time is unreal; the
flux of events is an illusion; they wish to withdraw into themselves and to be "alone with the
Alone."

The Indians, as we all know, are philosophers
of this school. They do not envy the European
and American, hustling and bustling like a squirrel
in a cage. As Matthew Arnold says:

> The East bowed low before the blast
> In patient deep disdain;
> She let the legions thunder past,
> And plunged in thought again.

He goes on to say that the "introvert" ideal came
in like a flood with Christianity, and filled the
deserts with monasteries and hermitages.

The "extraverts" are now having their innings.
Their achievements are for all to see. Not only has
material civilization won such triumphs as the
world has never seen before, but science has taught
us all to reverence fact and verification. When an
introvert tries to talk about science he flounders
terribly.

Hegel was a great philosopher; but this is his
contribution to the science of Heat. "Heat is the
self-restoration of matter in its formlessness, its

liquidity; the triumph of its abstract homogeneity over specific definiteness; its abstract, purely self-existing continuity as negation of negation is here set as activity." We need not puzzle our brains over this; there is no sense in it.

And yet, I sometimes remember a picture by Albrecht Dürer of *Melencolia*, as he spells it. Civilization is sitting pensive amid all her toys—very simple toys, we should think now!—and reflecting, "What is the good of it all?" The introvert who slumbers within us sometimes murmurs, "Why do ye spend your money on that which is not bread, and your labour on that which satisfieth not?"

In religion we have as two extreme types: the Catholic, for whom worship is a kind of charade or mystery-play, and the Quaker, who prefers to pray silently in a barn, that nothing may distract his thoughts.

For the former, dogma must concern itself with something which happened at a particular time and place. God must assert Himself by working miracles. All these things only disturb the mystic. If he accepts the historical element in religion, it is only as a symbol and sacrament of the super-historical. His favourite text about Christ is that He is "the same yesterday, to-day, and for ever."

The contrast between the two types is illustrated by comparing the words of Kant, "I only see what I think," with Goethe's "The sense of sight is that by which I best understand the outer world." Lord Kelvin, great scientist as he was, confessed that he must make a mechanical model before he could understand any physical theory.

I wonder whether most people remember by visualizing, as I do. When I forget a name, I recover it letter by letter, going through the alphabet till I find the letter which looks right. And I see numbers in printed letters before my mind's eye. Plato, I imagine, was a visualizer, for whom general "ideas" took shape as "forms" of beauty. The introvert is almost always a Platonist, the extravert an Aristotelian.

There are great disadvantages in being an extreme introvert, as I know to my cost. I constantly forget faces, and when a guide-book says, "It is impossible to miss your way from A to B," I can aver that it is quite possible, for I have done it.

Nevertheless, there are great compensations. I do not find that the extreme extravert has much intelligent enjoyment of the beauties of nature or art, or much appreciation of "the best that has been said and thought in the world." If he buys a mansion or a library or pictures, he values them only because they are his. He is a rather dull dog for all his success.

The success of the practical man may often be summed up in the words of the Psalmist, "He gave them their desire, and sent leanness withal into their soul."

The conclusion is that there is room for both types, and perhaps that the wise man lives sometimes in one world and sometimes in the other. For, after all, the outward and the inward must feed each other, or both will starve.

IV

THE CULT OF DIRT

DIRT has been defined as matter in the wrong place. It is not a very good definition. For instance, when I come back from a holiday, and find that the housemaid has been at my books, they are all in their wrong places, but not dirty; they are cleaner than before.

The word dirt implies a feeling of disgust. Metaphorically, we speak of a dirty book or dirty conduct, and all languages use the adjective metaphorically in much the same sense. It is difficult to analyse this feeling of disgust. It may be aroused by associations which affect some people and not others. A Roman Catholic lady, when a bishop introduced his wife, turned her back and exclaimed, "Dégoûtant!" A Hindu, after learning with horror that Englishmen actually put into their mouths an instrument made of the bone of a dog and the bristles of a pig, regarded our countrymen ever after as people of unutterably dirty habits.

For some obscure reason we dislike touching small living creatures—mice, rats, frogs and spiders —but this repulsion is often overcome. The dislike of vermin is much greater than it used to be, and has no doubt been increased by the fear of microbes. In the Middle Ages they did not mind. The cassock

146

of St. Francis was in an awful state, and so was the underclothing of St. Thomas à Becket. Cardinal Bellarmine would not allow his little guests to be disturbed, on the ground that, as they have no future life, they ought to be given a good time in this. Samuel Pepys and his wife, in the reign of Charles II, were "very merry" when they found that they had been sleeping in a lousy bed. Even now, in parts of South and East Europe, some of these little pests are taken philosophically. The fact is that wherever water is scarce cleanliness is difficult.

The deliberate cult of dirtiness as a thing pleasing to God is one of the most amazing things in social history, and makes us realize what a queer religion Christianity was fifteen hundred years ago.

No one will suggest that it has anything to do with real Christianity. It was part of a great ascetic movement, the beginnings of which can be traced in the first century, and which gradually captured the Church. It evidently sprang from deep psychological causes, which perhaps have not been fully explained.

A horror and disgust at the very idea of sex led those who aspired to the higher degrees of sanctity to hate their own bodies.

St. Francis, when he was dying prematurely of his austerities, confessed that he had been too hard upon "my brother the ass." The cleanliness of the body, as Lecky says, was regarded as a pollution

147

of the soul, and the saints who were most admired had become one hideous mass of clotted filth. St. Antony the hermit, says St. Athanasius with enthusiasm, never washed his feet. Abraham, another hermit, never washed his face either, and we are surprised to hear that "his countenance reflected the purity of his soul." Another saint had never seen himself naked.

We hear of a convent of a hundred and thirty nuns who shuddered at the mention of a bath. St. Augustine, who was a cultivated gentleman, advises his nuns to wash "at the usual intervals, that is to say, once a month." Jerome, while living as a hermit in Syria, tells us that his skin was covered with such a coating of dirt that he looked like a negro.

It would be easy to multiply evidence to the same effect. It does not matter much whether the stories of the habits of these ascetics were all true. The important thing is that for many centuries dirt was considered part of the highest moral excellence.

The impulse to do things because they are repulsive is often found both among Christian devotees and in other religions. In India the Aghorins dig up corpses and eat them. Mme Guyon, the French mystic, forced herself to eat—no matter what. But enough of this.

The hot-water tap has made a revolution in the practice of cleanliness. The daily cold-water tub, the last relic of Protestant asceticism, was a religious exercise, but I think it did not penetrate beyond the upper and professional classes. Certainly in the eighteenth century Dr. Johnson could say without shame, "I do not love immersion." And now we have doctors who tell us that we wash too much, and rub off a protecting layer from our skins. We cannot please the doctors anyhow.

The habit of sea and river bathing has increased enormously since the war in all parts of the world. It is not generally necessary for cleanliness; but it seems to mark a new feeling of pride in a healthy body such as has hardly been seen in Europe since the ancient Greeks.

We have learned, it seems, that cleanliness is next to godliness, at least in our persons. And our streets are beautifully clean, very unlike their horrible condition two hundred years ago and less. But what can we say of the air which our townsfolk breathe? The lungs of a Londoner, I am told, are dark grey; in manufacturing towns almost black. It is really rather humiliating to leave a Dutch or Scandinavian town, where everything looks spick and span, and come back to an English seaport.

We may expect that a hundred years hence some way of abating the smoke-nuisance will have been discovered. It is already, I suppose, better than it was fifty years ago, when London fogs were such as we seldom see now; but very much remains to be done. I was distressed to see that Athens, which two thousand years ago prided itself on its beautifully clear atmosphere, is now a dirty, smoky town. From the Piraeus one can only see the Acropolis through a haze; and the sulphuric acid in the air has completely ruined the Caryatides. Such is the penalty of industrialism; but some remedy must surely be found.

The most important thing, no doubt, is to clean the inside of the cup. "Unless a vessel is clean, whatever you pour into it turns sour," as Horace says. But it is worth while to make the outside clean also.

V

MIND IN THE MAKING

"MIND IN THE MAKING," by an American, J. H.
Robinson, is as good a shillingsworth as I ever
bought. It is recommended enthusiastically by
H. G. Wells, and I do not wonder, for it is the
pure milk of the Wellsian gospel.

How has man come to be as he is and to believe
what he does? Our knowledge of man, and of the
springs of his conduct, has lagged far behind our
progress in the natural sciences. We know that if
the majority of men thought as a few mostly unin-
fluential people now think, there would be no more
wars or revolutions.

But while a mechanic will mend a motor-car
efficiently and expeditiously, politicians are so much
in the dark about the true reasons why people act
and think as they do, that they give us little but
empty rhetoric and partisan appeals.

The human mind, says Mr. Wells, is essentially a
food-seeking system, and no better adapted for finding
the truth than the snout of a pig. We are incredibly
careless in forming our beliefs, but we become
passionately attached to them when anyone attacks
them. Most of our so-called reasoning consists in
finding arguments for going on believing as we do.

But most of our convictions are irrational; those
which we hold most strongly and tenaciously lie

so far back in human history that reason appeals
against them in vain. Such vital and fundamental
preoccupations as religion, love, war and the chase
were ingrained habits long before men began to use
their reason. "In all our reveries and speculations
we have three unsympathetic companions looking
on with jealous impatience—our wild apish progeni-
tor, a playful or peevish baby and a savage."

Can we liberate our intelligence from the ape,
the baby, and the savage? This is Mr. Robinson's
subject. His first rule is: When we find ourselves
convinced that our opinion is so certainly right that
to inquire into it would be unnecessary, or wicked,
or bad form, we may know that that opinion is
irrational, and probably founded upon inadequate
evidence.

Here I begin to have my doubts. It is quite true
that all taboo-morality is founded upon these
irrational and violent convictions, which in spite
of their absurdity are unassailable just because we
think it impious to question them. The horror which
a Hindu feels at the idea of killing a sacred cow,
a Moslem at the idea of eating pork, is proof against
all argument. The greased cartridges were really
a prime cause of the Indian Mutiny.

The belief that it is wicked to question authority
and tradition has been in truth the deadliest enemy
of progress. How many truth-seekers have been
silenced and intimidated we shall never know.

But I want to ask this question. Granting that

mere tradition is a bad reason for passing a verdict of true or false, right or wrong, on what grounds should the liberated intelligence give judgment? The weak point of scientific humanism is that it has no clear standard of right and wrong. Bentham's "greatest happiness of the greatest number" would, perhaps, still be accepted as a fair test.

But now, instead of thinking of absurd taboos, let us consider those deep-seated but unreasoned repugnances which we feel for certain actions or habits. I do not want to mention them, but let us think of the most disgusting practices we have ever heard of, and ask why they should be condemned by the dry light of reason. If we examine our own minds, we shall find that we condemn them because we know that they actually *are* disgraceful, and we do not wish to discuss the matter because we have reached bedrock.

Some things are absolutely right, others absolutely wrong, just as some things are really true, others false, some really beautiful, others ugly. The religious man believes that conscience is the voice of God within us, and that these convictions must be taken for what they seem to be, absolute and deeper than reason.

I will quote one maxim as a check upon Mr. Robinson's excellent argument. "Wise men, instead of exploding general prejudices, employ their sagacity to discover the latent wisdom which prevails in them" (Burke).

This caution in no way detracts from the value of Mr. Robinson's book. Religion, war and the chase may all be pre-rational habits, and yet we may hope to get rid of the second, and perhaps the third, without condemning the first.

Some ideas, which are doing endless harm, are very properly denounced by the author. Animism, for instance, is a very primitive superstition, which we may think we have outgrown. But we have not. It survives in one of the most noxious tendencies of the mind, one of the most virulent enemies of clear thinking—the habit of personification. It is impossible to exaggerate the mischief that has been done and is still being done by thinking and speaking of Germany, France, Italy, as if they were living persons, with good or (more often) very objectionable characteristics.

John Bull and Uncle Sam are as mythical as the great god Pan. We do not dislike Hans and Fritz when we meet them; but not long ago we were worked up to regard Germany as a demon, till we half believed that everyone who had the misfortune to be born between the Rhine and the Vistula had a double dose of original sin.

Partisanship is another great curse. We too readily assume that everything has two sides, and that it is our duty to be on one side or the other. We must always be defending or attacking some goal. Why are we so pugnacious?

VI

UGLINESS

I

OUR best philosophers—those at least whom I am proud to follow—tell us that the Creator reveals Himself to us under three attributes: Goodness, Truth and Beauty.

These are the absolute values, which exist in their own right. They cannot be explained by anything outside themselves. They cannot be reduced to anything else, or to each other, though they are inseparable, a threefold cord not quickly broken.

It is not a matter of taste whether we call things right or wrong, true or false, beautiful or ugly. They are so, once for all, and to call evil good or good evil is not a blunder but a blasphemy.

Negative values are a terrible problem for a philosopher. Shall we take the comfortable view that evil and ugliness are only a defect, a failure to achieve perfection? Are all deficiencies made good in the Absolute, whatever that may mean, so that we may say with Pope that all partial evil is universal good? Or shall we levy unlimited drafts on the future, like governments at war, and declare that the world, or mankind, or even God, is advancing towards perfection?

This leads to "inflation," a swelled head, and ends in repudiation. The moralist will have none of this whittling away of evil. He knows that there are negative temperatures far below zero. Rather than deny the reality of evil, he will believe in a personal devil.

Let us take the third of these absolute values, Beauty, and its opposite, Ugliness. I will explain presently why I have chosen the subject.

Beauty is the language in which the Creator speaks to us of Himself. Mankind has known the language three thousand years at least. We can read it in the book of nature, and in art; for artists know the language, which hardly changes at all. What was beautiful to the ancient Greeks and the medieval Italians is beautiful to us.

I do not agree that ugliness is absence of form or expression; it is false or vile expression.

The ugliest thing in nature, a human face distorted by evil passions, revolts us because the evil principle has set its mark on what was meant to bear the image of God. There is nothing ugly in what only wants cleaning, like a fine picture covered with dirt; our characters need something more drastic than soap and water to make them beautiful.

Apart from human sin, is there anything ugly in nature?

The grotesque is not ugly. I cannot help thinking

that the Creator made some animals, and some human beings, just for fun. The elephant, the hippopotamus, the baboon with blue cheeks and scarlet stern, are not ugly; they are figures of comedy. Why should not the Deity have a sense of humour?

A few animals, such as the crocodile, which seems to belong to a museum of dinosaurs, the shark and the octopus, are horrible, and horror is akin to a sense of ugliness, though not quite the same. Why certain harmless animals cause us *disgust* is a difficult psychological question.

Besides this, nature, for some inscrutable reason, has associated the beginning and end of life with mechanisms which, though right and proper, are felt to be either humiliating or terrible.

If it were not so familiar to us, we should think it a cruel insult that we have to hide away the earthly casket of an immortal soul before "decay's effacing fingers" begin to ravage it, and that it is a shame to speak of the manner in which nature brought us into the world. But so it is; to offend against these decencies is to be unfit for civilized society.

And yet I read that one of our modern critics, contrasting Baudelaire with Tennyson, singles out for special praise that worst poem of Baudelaire, which describes the swarming of flies and maggots on a woman's putrid corpse, and explains that *In Memoriam* fails because Tennyson failed to picture

Arthur Hallam lying like that in Clevedon churchyard!

As for the other theme, in which reserve has hitherto been considered proper, the same scholar to whom I owe this last illustration, in a lecture to the British Academy, says, not a bit too strongly: "Our own generation has made a god of its own likeness out of D. H. Lawrence; for that typical victim of its own diseases—of its industrialism, its barbarism, its brutal love of shouting on the housetops what sensible people have always known and never said—had the gift of words to make men listen."

A very popular novel by another hero of our new critics is described by Mr. Noyes as the foulest that has ever found its way into print. I have not read it myself. Such outrages against decency, which have nothing to do with the comparatively harmless ribaldry of Aristophanes and Rabelais, are a deliberate cult of ugliness, a new and vile symptom of European decadence.

New we may call it; but Robert Louis Stevenson fifty years ago saw what was coming, and the effect it would have on literature and its traditions. "The British pig returns to his true love, the love of the styleless, of the shapeless, of the slapdash, and the disorderly. There is trouble coming, I think." It has come.

There is only one language of beauty, though there are different dialects. We know it in nature,

UGLINESS

II

GOOD style, says Mr. Yeats, is purification from insincerity, vanity, malignity and arrogance. It is just high breeding in words and argument. The words "high breeding" give us the test which we want, and I have no doubt that an instinctive hatred of high breeding, a sort of inverted snobbery or intellectual Bolshevism, inspires some of the worst outrages against good taste.

To describe the condition of a putrefying corpse, like Baudelaire, or an outcast woman dying of confluent small-pox, like Zola; to picture in detail, like Zola again, the behaviour of a bull with a cow; to write a poem about being sick, or, like one of the American leaders of this school, about a man tearing his shirt with "a ripping razzly noise," is a deliberate insult to decency and human dignity.

The source of it is, I imagine, a malignant hatred of all accepted values, or sometimes a contempt for human nature, which is to be exhibited naked and disgusting. There is a morbid strain in some of these writers.

These apostles of a new culture have formed a

mutual admiration clique. They have captured several of our leading newspapers. The word "genius" can never be omitted in speaking of some dirty novelist, some painter who can neither draw nor paint, some poet whose verses neither scan nor make sense.

In sculpture, we are told that "essential sculpture has the same kind of meaning as the sphere, the cube, and the cylinder."

It is possible that a great mathematician might find poetry in a cube or a cylinder, as the Pythagoreans did in the regular pentagon, the construction of which (no mean feat in those days) they discovered. But to ask us to prefer Euclid's picture of the ass's bridge to the Rialto or old Waterloo Bridge is going a bit too far.

Is there any obscure connection between this taste for diagrams in art and the tendency in modern physics to reduce all reality to mathematical symbols? If God, as Sir James Jeans thinks, is a mathematician, can it be that He likes His churches to be built in "cubes and cylinders," and would prefer Madonnas to be painted with green hair?

I do not believe it for a moment. The Creator is a supreme artist and poet, and He speaks to us in the language which artists and poets learned thousands of years ago, and have been speaking ever since.

"Reversion to the primitive type," says a biologist, "is always the prelude to extinction." So there is hope that golliwogism in art may be a symptom of a fatal disease which will carry its victims into nothingness and oblivion. But I sometimes fear that Spengler's prophecy, *The Decline of the West*, may be only too true.

The revolutionary is always trying to build a tree, which cannot be done, especially as he wants to build it without roots.

I know what these critics say—that the great schools of art and literature have achieved all that can be done on those lines. Every art can develop until it reaches its culmination, and no further. Greek sculpture reached one kind of perfection; are we merely to copy it, knowing that our copies must always be inferior to the originals?

So with architecture and painting, and even with poetry. We cannot surpass Raphael or Milton or the builders of Chartres. Are we to be only laughed at and abused if we try something new?

By all means let them try something new. I can admire some of the skyscrapers of New York, and still more the new town hall at Stockholm. I appreciate the brutal but effective swagger of the railway station at Milan.

There may be successful new experiments in painting and sculpture, and in music, which I, unluckily, do not understand. But this plea does not touch what I have been saying about deliberate ugliness.

An age of science ought, we are sometimes told,

163

to have its distinctive forms of art. Some would add that an age of equality ought to have its own art. But this is difficult. Uniformity is always really ugly. Compare an old-fashioned village, such as that where I live, with the monotonous rows of small houses, all exactly alike, which are now springing up.

A countryside spotted all over with bungaloid growths must make an artist sigh for the bad old times when the rich man in his castle lived in a noble park, and the poor man at his gate had a picturesque black and white cottage which, externally at least, was a thing of beauty.

As for a possible alliance between Science and Beauty, was there any symbolic meaning in that unfortunate scandal on Olympus, described by Homer?

Aphrodite (Venus), the goddess of love and beauty, was the wife of Hephaestus (Vulcan), a very able practical scientist, but unhappily lame and rather dirty. Aphrodite was unfaithful to him, and had an affair with Ares (Mars), the dashing and handsome war-god. Hephaestus found them together; he enclosed them in a net, and invited all the gods and goddesses to come and see. The gods came and enjoyed the joke hugely; but "the lady-goddesses," says Homer, "remained each in her house for shame."

Well, is there any chance that Hephaestus, no longer lame or dirty, may make it up with Aphro-

164

dite, now that Mars, as we hope, will soon be permanently caged, or expelled from Olympus?

Some will say that I take these exhibitions of bad taste far too seriously. They may be only a passing fashion. But if our age is really resolved to heap scorn on all that mankind have loved and admired since they began to find in Beauty a vision of God, we must be prepared for what in very old-fashioned language was called the coming of Antichrist.

SOCIAL

I

OTHER PEOPLE'S PLEASURES

I REMEMBER reading an amusing story called *In the Wrong Paradise*. What worse Purgatory could there be than to be sent to enjoy oneself among people of totally different tastes? Life would be tolerable, someone has said, if it were not for its amusements. "How many things there are that I don't want," a philosopher remarked after being taken to a luxurious house.

We all have our likes and dislikes, and I confess that some people's tastes are quite incomprehensible to me. Here are a few of them.

1. *Killing animals.* I have never killed anything larger than a wasp, and that was in self-defence. I once took a poker to a rat in the deanery study, but was rather glad when I missed him. I am not a vegetarian, and quite realize that no one has so much interest in the demand for pork as the pig. If we were all Jews, there would soon be no pigs left. But what possible pleasure can there be in curtailing the lives of our pretty and harmless cousins in fur and feathers?

Dr. Johnson was once persuaded to have a day in the hunting-field. His friends expected him to fall off, but though the lexicographer did not know the meaning of "pastern," he knew how to sit tight. At the end of the day he said pensively, "Sir, it illustrates the paucity of human pleasures that this should be reckoned as one of them."

This judgment will be received with contempt and indignation by many excellent people who have no murderous feelings against foxes. But I think if I were a headmaster, I should face unpopularity by abolishing the school beagles. It cannot be good for a boy to see a hare "broken up."

As for big game shooting, there is no doubt a spice of danger. But it is disgusting to hear of the wild beasts being run down by motor-cars. If a lion is to have a fair chance, why not hunt him like Asshurbanipal, King of Assyria, whose exploits may be studied in the British Museum? The monarch stands in a kind of wheelbarrow drawn by two horses, and shoots ferocious lions at close quarters with a bow and arrow. Asshurbanipal was a real sportsman.

Another plan would be to issue licences to sportsmen to stalk and shoot each other. That would be really exciting; the sportsman might then adorn his hall with scalps, instead of stags' heads and tiger skins.

2. *Mountaineering.* If there is any occupation which combines in its acutest form every element of discomfort—cold, heat, fatigue and danger—it is climbing a mountain. Most mountains look their best from below; and if they do not there is the funicular railway up many of them. As *one* version

of a popular hymn says: "They climbed the steep ascent of heaven, with peril, toil and pain; but oh! to me may sense be given, to follow by the train."

However, I know several clergymen and schoolmasters who choose this kind of holiday. Perhaps it helps them "always to take the highest ground." But it is a sad pity when they break their necks, for many valuable lives have been lost in this way.

3. *Dancing.* "Hardly anyone dances when he is sober, unless he is insane," says Cicero. I do not think I should wish to dance even if I were drunk. I believe a passion for dancing is always one of the sequelæ of a great war; it was noticed after the French Revolution. But what surprises me is the lugubrious shuffle which our young people call dancing. To judge by their other habits in the 'twenties, I should have expected them to choose an orgiastic style of dancing, like the French cancan (which I believe was a perfectly proper dance), or the Greek cordax (which was not).

4. There are one or two feminine pleasures which I cannot be expected to understand. *Aimless chattering*, for example. The railway companies, poor things, are very enterprising just now. Let them give up non-smoking carriages, since nobody minds tobacco now, and mark their compartments "Talkers" and "Non-Talkers." In non-talking carriages passengers would, of course, be allowed to speak when they had something to say; but

inveterate chatterers would have to travel in the cars allotted to them.

5. *Watching ceremonies.* What possible pleasure can there be in watching total strangers getting married, or buried, which seems to be even more popular? Occasionally one sees a man outside a church at a wedding, but he seems to be saying to himself: "But for the grace of Providence, there goes ——" whatever his name may be. But why do the women go? Is it to see another victim led to the altar?

Such are a few of the pleasures which I am glad to avoid. Of course I have my own, plenty of them.

Books are an inexhaustible fountain of enjoyment. And oh, the joy of being now "on the shelf," and able to browse in my library without any ulterior object!

Next to reading, I should put cruising. I have five times enjoyed the hospitality of Sir Henry Lunn on his Mediterranean cruises, and I know no more delightful holiday. My heart leaps up when I behold the deep blue waters of the Mediterranean. (But why in the world does everyone quote Homer's "wine-dark sea" as if it were a beautiful epithet? It is true that Homer was blind, but he must have known that no wine ever looked like the sea. The Greeks did not drink crême de menthe. Perhaps he only meant "foaming," as Greek wine probably did.)

I am of course much too old to play games,

172

and I was never very keen about any except cricket and lawn-tennis. Lawn-tennis is the ideal game to watch. The interest never flags, and the spectators are near enough to see everything. I used to enjoy watching first-class cricket, but I no longer care for it. The game is not what it was. The bat has beaten the ball; and the practice of using the legs as a second line of defence is not only unsportsmanlike and unfair to the bowler; it has spoilt some of the prettiest strokes of the game. Unless the M.C.C. takes vigorous action, I think the popularity of our national game will soon decline.

This is a frivolous article. I have said nothing of the deeper sources of happiness, such as friendship and family affection, and the sacred assurance which comes to us at times, that we can enjoy the blessedness of communion with the Author of our being. These are not to be discussed among the amusements and recreations of life. Among the lighter pleasures it is, perhaps, wise to choose one or two which will not fail us in old age, and among these something better than crossword puzzles and bridge. Some hobby is very useful. However small an object of interest may appear when we look at it superficially, it becomes interesting when we go deeper into it. It is for this reason that a narrow sphere does not necessarily cramp a broad mind.

II

THE GENTLEMAN

In an excellent little book just published, called
Money, Morals and Manners, by H. V. Routh, the
last chapter is headed "The Passing of the Gentleman." The author thinks that the word is now
used only by hall-porters, shop-assistants and a few
women. This is surely an exaggeration, though I
have noticed a tendency to use certain odious
synonyms, of which "a white man" is the worst.
As if a brown, red, yellow or black man could not
be a gentleman!

Culture, Mr. Routh thinks, is in search of a new
character-type. The old type was based on an
ancient and honourable culture—the Bible, the
classics, the literature of the Renaissance. (I do not
think it was really based on books to any great
extent.) The new type is based on intellectual
independence and technical skill, a combination,
we might say, of H. G. Wells and a glorified
chauffeur like Bernard Shaw's 'Enry Straker.
Straker has no respect for a gentleman as such;
he prefers his own class.

There is no doubt a democratic revolt against
any assumption of superiority. Even in speech, the
disdain long expressed by the gentry for a Cockney
or provincial accent is now turned against their

own way of speaking English. The shibboleths of class are no longer to be respected.

But these are superficial signs. I do not think that any new ideal of character has supplanted the old. On the contrary, I think that the new ideal of equality of consideration has purified and refined the idea of a gentleman, by stripping it of adventitious accessories which went far to spoil it.

Ever since the age of Elizabeth, when the ideal of the national character first became explicit, there is abundant evidence that Englishmen knew very well what the word gentleman meant, and that it has nothing essential to do with heraldry, property in land or the existence of a leisured class.

Of course the good old word has been shamefully abused. I can remember when it often meant simply a man who does not work for his living. Lord Chesterfield thought that Dr. Johnson was no gentleman because he treated his superiors, equals and inferiors all alike. George IV said, "Peel is no gentleman. He divides his coat-tails when he sits down." Perhaps the worst definition is that "a gentleman is never *unintentionally* rude."

Dean Church says truly that the ideal, as we see it first, perhaps, in Spenser's *Faerie Queene*, was a new character in the world. It had not really existed in the days of feudalism and chivalry, which were too wild, coarse and turbulent. "To birth and capacity must be added a new delicacy of conscience, a new appreciation of what is beautiful and worthy of honour, a new measure of the strength and nobleness of self-control, of devotion to unselfish interests."

It was something which on the same scale had not been seen yet, and which was to be the seed of something greater. "It was to grow into that high type of cultivated English nature, than which our western civilization has produced few things more admirable."

It would be easy to show by quotations that intelligent foreigners have recognized this lay religion of the English as one of the noblest ideals in the world, and the source of what is most praiseworthy in our national character. We owe to it our incorruptible magistrates, our habitual fairness, our instinct to help the weak and to hurry to the post of danger, our respect for speaking the truth, our dislike for tortuous and underhand procedures.

It is precisely because these are not characteristics of any one class that we do not use the word so much as our fathers did; there still hangs about it a suspicion of exclusiveness. But the absence of these qualities, the character which we sum up by the ugly word "cad," is as much the unpardonable sin in England as it ever was.

Thirty years ago Professor W. H. Garrod wrote a most arresting essay called "Christian, Greek or Goth?" He asks the question from what source

176

we get our national ideal of the perfect character. From the Old Testament? Hardly. "Jacob have I loved, and Esau have I hated." But we prefer Esau. David, the man after God's own heart? How about his conduct to Michal, Abner, Uriah and Shimei? But Mr. Garrod might have remembered (in the Old Testament) the Fifteenth Psalm; and surely anyone who modelled his conduct on the Sermon on the Mount or on the thirteenth chapter of I Corinthians would pass the most exacting standard of gentlemanliness.

Our lay religion is not Hebraic. Is it then Greek? (Matthew Arnold regarded these two types as the only alternatives.) The wily Ulysses, with a wife in every port and a lie for every emergency, clearly would not do as a national hero. Aristotle's "great-souled man," who "thinks himself worthy of great things and is worthy of them," is, as Mr. Garrod says, rather like a nobleman in a novel by Disraeli, but not like any other kind of gentleman.

No; our week-day ideal does not come from Palestine nor from Athens. Nor does it come from the Catholic Church, though there are many fine gentlemen in England who were born and bred in the old faith. Cardinal Newman's famous delineation of a gentleman recognizes that it is an alien type. He quite untruly makes it depend mainly on polished manners, cool indifference, and pride.

Where, then, did we find our ideal? Mr. Garrod says we are Goths. We live, or wish to live, by the Northern European code of honour, which is independent of the classical tradition. But what about chivalry? Was there none in the Latin countries? Certainly there was, after Southern Europe had been overrun by the barbarians. The Crusades, and chivalry, were a strange importation into Christianity, and they were inspired by northern, not Mediterranean, ideas.

I am inclined to think that chivalry was not really Christian—I mean chivalry as it actually existed. Spenser dressed it up in Elizabethan costume, and Tennyson, taking still greater liberties, turned Arthur and his knights into very decent Victorian gentlemen. But they did not behave quite like that in the Middle Ages.

I think Mr. Garrod is partly right. We instinctively feel ourselves nearer to Scandinavians and Dutchmen and Germans, at any rate to South Germans and Austrians, than to the Latin races. We are partly "Goths," and the idea of a gentleman is partly, not wholly, Gothic.

But I cannot admit that Christianity is a stranger outside the Mediterranean region. I think it was meant to be a universal religion, and Northern Europe has its own very valuable contribution to make in bringing out all that there is in it.

At any rate, the best man that England can produce is a good Englishman, and I hope we shall

178

never think of discarding the finest flower of our national culture, though perhaps we may prefer not to talk much about it. There are some virtues, like humility and purity, which are spoilt by thinking about them, and perhaps the perfect gentleman is unconscious that he is one.

III

SIN AND CRIME

IF I were made dictator, I think I should employ the short interval between my appointment and my assassination in overhauling the criminal law, which seems to me to have lagged far behind what any intelligent person would wish to see.

To a large extent the law is no doubt controlled by public opinion. Juries will not convict if their sympathies are strongly with the prisoner. But public opinion is also influenced by the law, and sometimes, I venture to think, mischievously

The most salient example is murder. A hundred years ago there was a long list of capital offences; now murder and high treason alone remain. There is a confused idea that the Old Testament sanctions the execution of murderers and of murderers only. The truth is that under the Mosaic law many other offences, including adultery and Sabbath breaking, were punished by stoning.

The result in the change in our criminal law is that murder is popularly regarded as on a different footing from any other crime. Writers of detective stories almost always choose murder as their subject; the public is only mildly interested in anything else. The police, when they are not shepherding pedestrians across the streets, are engaged in hunting down murderers.

The public takes a ghoulish delight in these "mysteries"; and when the culprit is found, he is hounded to his fate with a callousness greater than that of the Roman populace at a gladiatorial show. The mode of execution is humane; the moral cruelty of the publicity is monstrous.

I have not the slightest sympathy with the agitation against capital punishment. The State is quite within its rights in weeding out thoroughly undesirable citizens. But our manner of doing it is barbarous and unjust.

If the authorities judge a malefactor to be incurable, he ought to be humanely extinguished without any publicity, and without casting any stigma on his name or family. The capital sentence ought not to be attached to murder only. Many murderers are by no means incorrigible criminals; many burglars are so.

I shall never forget seeing a batch of prisoners just released from Stafford Gaol; they were on the platform of the railway station. Several of them were "fellows by the hand of nature marked, quoted and signed to do some deed of shame." No one would employ them; they were simply turned loose to prey upon society, which no doubt they proceeded to do. The absurdity of our prison system was borne in upon me irresistibly.

In all ancient codes, offences against God were

punished as crimes. There was no distinction between sin and crime. Theoretically we now hold that the law does not punish sin. But in practice it does.

Some kinds of immorality excite repugnance among decent people, and they are still punished by long terms of imprisonment, though the culprit is usually allowed twenty-four hours to fly from the country.

Other kinds of immorality, such as adultery, which in many old codes was a capital offence, are not punished at all. The result is that offences of the former class, which are often caused by mental abnormality, are regarded with horror, while the shameful sin of adultery is condoned.

It would be better, I think, to protect the young of both sexes, and to remove offences of this kind committed by adults from the jurisdiction of the criminal courts.

In revolutionary Russia any sign of disaffection against the State is punished with death, but the maximum penalty for murder is a few years of imprisonment. On the other hand, in some countries political assassins often find much sympathy. I can see no justification for treating political conspirators with leniency.

Another curious survival of the notion that the State ought to punish sin is the attitude of the State towards suicide, which is still a crime in our law, though not, I believe, in any other civilized country.

From the legal as opposed to the religious point of view I think a man has a right to declare his innings closed; and I should always give a criminal the option of carrying out his sentence upon himself.

Another manifest absurdity is to put on his trial for murder a doctor who has accidentally caused the death of a patient while performing an illegal operation. He ought to be punished, no doubt, but not as a homicide. Nothing was further from his intention than to kill his patient.

It is a nice question how far the sympathies of the judge and jury ought to influence the verdict and sentence. We do not wish to see the emotional appeals which in France often gain acquittal for the perpetrator of "un crime passionel," and some considerations, such as the good looks of a female prisoner, are certainly illegitimate. The admission of women to juries, has, I am told, unmasked many seductive female malefactors.

Behind all discussion of reforms in criminal procedure lies the question whether it is right to punish at all—a favourite topic in school and college debating societies. It is not very difficult to straighten this matter out.

There are three possible motives for inflicting a penalty on a criminal—the hope of reforming him; the wish to deter others from doing the same thing; and the wish to hurt the criminal because we think it right that he should be hurt. The last is in my opinion the only legitimate use of the word punishment. Reformatory treatment is not punishment because it happens to be unpleasant. Surgical operations are generally unpleasant, but we do not call them punishment. The motive of deterrence is only justifiable as an act of self-protection by the State against its potential enemies. Punishment in the proper sense is always and essentially vindictive. The criminal law, as St. Paul says, is an avenger to execute wrath upon him that doeth evil.

We have become much more merciful since the days when descriptions of the torments of hell resounded from every pulpit. But is the desire to see justice done upon the transgressor an unworthy feeling? I cannot think so. Take a case of horrible cruelty to a child or even to an animal; or of a man bribed to betray his country in time of war; or of cold-blooded seduction; or of poisoning.

Surely we wish to see the offender suffering condign chastisement; and if he is too bad to be reformed, that is certainly no reason for letting him off.

I observe that in almost all these questions I generally have the Socialists against me. This does not make me at all more inclined to alter my opinion.

IV

LOVE AND MARRIAGE

PROFESSOR WESTERMARCK, our greatest authority on marriage law and custom in all parts of the world, has now written a very interesting book on *The Future of Marriage in Western Civilization* (Macmillan, 12s. 6d.).

He has no doubt that the institution of marriage and the family is not seriously threatened; it is an integral part of civilization. Communists wish to destroy it; it is much more likely to destroy Communism.

The causes for which marriage was ordained are correctly summed up in the Anglican marriage service, in a sentence which horrified Victorian prudishness. The third cause—"mutual society, help and comfort"—is strongly emphasized by Westermarck, who is no sentimentalist, and who does not write as a Christian.

The notion that husband and wife must tend to drift apart when they are no longer passionately in love with each other is quite untrue. The deep affection which a happily married couple feel for each other is quite independent of what the Prayer Book calls carnal appetite; Westermarck even says, I believe quite truly, that "in a young person's first love this desire is often completely absent; indeed the thought of it may fill him with reluctance"; and "when this attraction has ceased to be felt, its spiritual effect may still remain unabated."

One feels almost ashamed of emphasizing such an obvious truth; but advocates of free love or of easy divorce have said and written so much about the sacredness of physical passion that protests are very much needed.

One of their arguments is that most marriages are unhappy. Statistics are hardly obtainable; but it is obvious that happy marriages do not get into the newspapers.

I am inclined to guess that the proportion arrived at by a New York physician, Dr. Hamilton, is probably near the mark. He asked a hundred married men and a hundred married women this question: "If by some miracle you could press a button and find that you had never been married to your husband or wife, would you press the button?"

One hundred and thirty out of the two hundred said "No"; sixteen said "No, with qualification"; only twenty-eight said "Yes."

Considering the tendency of human nature to be discontented with what we have got, I think that is a very high percentage of success.

Swift cynically said that "the reason why so few marriages are happy is that young ladies spend their time in making nets, not in making cages." Bernard

Shaw has tried to persuade us that woman is the hunter, man the hunted. But the nicest girls do not make nets, and do not need to make cages.

Do love-marriages turn out better than those which are made partly at least from other motives?

Westermarck quotes from a German writer: "No choice is ever all for love or all for convenience. Even in love there is a valuation of the partner, and beneath the blindness of love there is often much calculation." Where there is none, I am disposed to think that the risks are great.

Montaigne says: "I see no marriages which sooner fail than those contracted on account of beauty and amorous desires."

That is the one argument against early marriage. The young man is apt to marry a pretty face, especially when its owner is clever at "making nets"; the couple may prove to be quite unsuited to each other.

Disraeli went so far as to say: "All my friends who have married for love and beauty either beat their wives or live apart from them. This is literally the case. I may commit many follies in life, but I never intend to marry for love, which I am sure is a guarantee of infelicity."

He did not marry for love; he made a prudent alliance with an excellent but rather unattractive lady, who had money.

Mrs. Disraeli had no illusions about it. "Dizzy did not marry me for love," she said; "but he would now." When someone took the liberty of expressing surprise at Disraeli's devotion to his wife, he replied, "I have a reason which few people understand— gratitude." It was a perfect marriage.

Can there be a happy marriage without jealousy?

It is an ugly passion, no doubt. A prison commissioner has found that more murders are committed from jealousy than from any other single cause. But we should think poorly of any husband who was indifferent to his wife's unfaithfulness. Wives are sometimes more accommodating; what they fear most is that their husbands should cease to love them.

The French are quite convinced that their system of arranging marriages by the parents of the young people is better than ours, of leaving the young people to choose for themselves.

Of course the difference is not really so sharp as that. I think that in France the young people usually know each other fairly well before they are engaged; and with us the parents, in the upper and middle classes, have a good deal to say in the matter.

The French marriage is, I believe, generally successful. Madame is an excellent partner. She cooks her husband's dinner admirably, or sees that the cook does so; she keeps his accounts and saves his francs, and manages to look nice. What more can a Frenchman wish for?

The German *Hausfrau*, though less attractive,

is equally efficient, and since Hitler came into power she has one conspicuous merit. A friend of mine, to my surprise, came back from Germany an ardent Hitlerite. His explanation was, "All the time I was there I did not see a single woman with a painted face. Hitler has stopped all that." (Since then I have heard that he has not been able to stop it!)

Nevertheless, unless continental fiction is very misleading, disgraceful "triangles" are much more common than with us, where love is presupposed and generally exists.

Shakespeare's glorious sonnet, "Let me not to the marriage of true minds," sums up all that one wishes to say on this subject. Married love, if it is the real thing, increases with the years, because it is based on friendship and affection. And for those who are contemplating marriage, I have one word of advice: not *Punch's* "Don't," nor Socrates' "Whichever way you decide, you will regret it"; but this:

A man is a good judge of his own sex, a bad judge of the other; and the same is true of a girl. The worst mistakes would be avoided if a young man was careful to choose a girl who has good women for her friends, and if a girl was careful to choose a man who is liked and respected by good men.

I believe I have said this before, but it is such good advice that I am not ashamed to repeat it.

V

FEAR OF DEATH

THERE is a curious verse in one of the noblest books of the New Testament, the Epistle to the Hebrews. Christ submitted to death, says the writer, "to deliver them who through fear of death were all their lifetime subject to bondage."

Have we ever known anyone who was tormented in this way by the fear of death? Were people more afraid of death two thousand years ago than they are now? This is an interesting question for a classical scholar, and for a social historian.

There is some reason to think that they were so. Lucretius wrote his great poem to free mankind from fear of the gods, and from fear of death. His denunciation of the fear of death is one of the most magnificent parts of his book. There is no after life, he says (being an Epicurean), and therefore there is nothing to feel and nothing to fear.

"Enjoy your life, unconscionable man, and go to sleep when your time comes." This was the comfortable, sensible, unheroic philosophy of his sect.

But Seneca, who was a Stoic, also argues against the fear of death in a way which implies that it was almost universal. "All," he says, "young, middle-aged and old, are equally afraid of death," and Cicero says the same.

Would any modern be craven enough to write the lines which alone survive of Maecenas, the great statesman and patron of Virgil and Horace? "Make me a cripple in hand, foot and back; make me a hunchback and toothless; while life is in me, I am well; keep me alive, even on the cross."

How far the fear of hell has terrified the dying under Christianity it is very difficult to say. I do not think that the clergy often encounter it now. But Dr. Johnson, who had less to be sorry for than nine men out of ten, was genuinely afraid that he would be sent to hell; this was the source of the fear of death which he frankly confessed. We might have supposed that the awful pictures of eternal punishment which were accepted without demur until quite recently would have added greatly to the fear of death; for it has been the teaching of the Church that only a small minority escape them. Of the majority it may be said in Dante's terrible words, "These have no *hope* of death." But the effect of this teaching has been so small, either in deterring men from sin or in filling their last hours with horror, that we must conclude that it was never believed very heavily.

Most people, when they come to die, are ready to commend their spirits to a God whom they believe to be both just and merciful; and though they have done many things which they are very sorry for, they do not think that they deserve to be tortured for ever.

Whether people were really more afraid of death in antiquity must be left in doubt. In the Middle Ages St. Francis wrote a beautiful hymn to "Sister Death"; and a very different brand of poet, Walt Whitman, laid aside his "barbaric yawp" to compose a really noble welcome to death.

From my own observation, I should say that there is not much fear of death among us now. The courage of the soldiers in the Great War, in circumstances far more trying than the old cavalry charge, is undisputed.

Sometimes one meets infinitely pathetic cases, like that of Charlotte Brontë, whose last words were: "I cannot be going to die; we have been so happy together." But usually the young, especially, surrender the cup which they have hardly tasted with a calm serenity which is one of the most splendid and awe-inspiring things in human life.

Those whose work is done are generally fairly well content to go. If they are believers, they say: "Lord, now lettest Thou Thy servant depart in peace"; if not, they say with Victor Hugo: "C'est la mort. Elle est la bienvenue."

But "last words" are not worth the importance which is given to them. We shall never know whether Pitt expired with the words: "My country, how I leave my country!" or whether he merely remarked: "I should like one of Bellamy's pies."

But if we are not much afraid of death, we are

very much afraid of what may come before it. "Pour être mort," said the Frenchman, "malheureusement il faut mourir." To put it plainly, we are all so horribly afraid of dying of cancer that it is bad manners to mention the word except in a whisper. It is this secret terror, very well founded, I am sorry to say, which has revived the old appeal that euthanasia may in some cases be legalized.

Lewis Nettleship, the Oxford philosopher, who met his own death in the Alps with great courage and cheerfulness, used to say, "Death does not count."

This is the way in which a brave man should regard it. It is a law, not a punishment.

VI

EUTHANASIA

IF I refuse to put a mangled horse or dog out of its misery, I may be fined for cruelty. If I help a human being, who is dying horribly by inches from cancer, gangrene, or locomotor ataxy, to shorten his or her sufferings, from which there can be no release but death, I may be hanged for murder. Such is the law, which the late Lord Moynihan and many others have wished to change. But it is impossible to allow the relatives of an invalid, without his or her consent, to take the law into their own hands. If euthanasia is to be permitted in certain cases, every precaution against abuse must be taken.

I have tried to make up my mind on this difficult question. As a Christian, ought I to condemn euthanasia absolutely as contrary to the revealed law of God? The opposition of religion is the most formidable obstacle which those who advocate a change in the law have to meet.

There is no doubt that the majority of religious people condemn the proposal. Putting aside those for whom the question has been decided by an authority which they are forbidden to call in question, two arguments are often used in favour of maintaining the existing practice.

First, we are told that pain and suffering are ordained by God, and that we have no right to refuse to bear them. Texts from the Old Testament are still sometimes adduced as authoritative. For instance, we read in Genesis that women must bear children "in sorrow." Queen Victoria and many of her subjects refused the aid of narcotics when they were bringing their numerous children into the world. It was in vain that they were reminded that according to the same authority God gave Adam an anæsthetic when He extracted his rib. The answer was: "True; but He never gave one to Eve." This objection has ceased to carry weight for intelligent Christians.

It is almost absurd to suppose that the Creator ← allowed so many ways of mitigating suffering to exist and to be discovered, but forbade the use of them. Pain patiently borne no doubt ennobles the character, but that is no reason why we should not use every means of reducing or removing it; it seems unlikely that unnecessary cruelty can be part of the will of God.

The other objection is that euthanasia is suicide, and that suicide is not only a deadly sin, but, from the nature of the case, is a sin of which it is impossible to repent. According to the traditional teaching of the Church, a soul dying in deadly sin is lost. Such a mechanical test as this is quite contrary to our ideas of justice, and we really cannot believe in it. We shall be judged on

195

our lives as a whole, not by the state of mind we happen to be in when death overtakes us. And though I should always do my best to dissuade a friend from taking his own life, I am not prepared to say that it is our duty always to keep the breath in our bodies till the last gasp.

So long as we can do any good in the world it is our duty to live on, even though we may be suffering and unhappy; and I know that many persons who suffer from incurable sickness give a beautiful example of patience, cheerfulness and resignation which is of great spiritual value. But does this cover all cases? I think not.

We very properly hide away the most distressing cases of illness, and many people do not know how horrible the preliminaries of death sometimes are. In order to help myself to form an intelligent opinion on this question, I spent an hour in the museum of the Royal College of Surgeons, and purposely looked at the most dreadful among the exhibits. What I saw made my blood run cold. It was far worse than the old dungeon at The Hague, with all the instruments of torture in working order. The most diabolical cruelties of man pale before the torments which Nature sometimes inflicts upon her innocent victims. Even the Inquisition seldom went on torturing people for months. And now that all civilized nations have abolished judicial torture, and think of it with horror, can we face with equanimity the worse cruelties which thousands every year have to undergo at the hands of Nature, and say confidently, all this is the will of God?

If we talk to medical men, who know the facts as others seldom know them, we almost always find that they are dissatisfied with the rule which the ethics of their profession oblige them to obey—that their duty is to keep the patient alive, by every possible means, till the last moment. Nature left to herself would be more merciful; it is the artificial and unnatural prolongation of life in terrible pain which they feel to be sheer cruelty.

And yet, though all the arguments seem to be strongly in favour of the proposed change in the law, I could not bring myself to add my name to the signatures in favour of Lord Moynihan's Bill. For consider a very typical case—the commonest case, probably, that would arise if the Bill became law. A woman is suffering from inoperable cancer. The doctor reluctantly informs her that she will probably live for some months in dreadful pain, and perhaps with those repulsive symptoms which often accompany the later stages of the disease. On hearing this, she asks for euthanasia. Her written request has to be countersigned by her nearest relative—her husband. He is asked to give his consent to the curtailment of his wife's earthly existence by some months; to antedate the inevitable parting; to forgo the tender ministrations in which the great love of a lifetime might find its last expression; to sign the death-warrant of his nearest and dearest. Can one imagine a more horrible dilemma?

My position, I confess, is rather illogical. But in a question like this, natural feelings cannot be disregarded. The human spirit can often triumph over pain with a quiet heroism which amazes the onlookers. Those who have seen many deathbeds would only rarely, I think, wish that they had been anticipated by an overdose of morphia.

I am inclined to think that if the proposed Bill passes into law,* it will not be taken advantage of very often. Perhaps this is the best solution. Euthanasia should be permitted, but only in very exceptional cases.

* It has now been rejected by the House of Lords.

VII

A WORLD OF ROBOTS

I HAVE been reading a book called *New Minds for Old*, by Esme Wingfield-Stratford, a writer for whom I have a great admiration, increased, perhaps, by the fact that he is an old Etonian and a Fellow of my college. He wants us all to train our bodies and minds more systematically so as to get the best out of ourselves, and he gives us good advice how to do it.

I am afraid, however, that he is much too optimistic when he says on the last page that "not mediocrity but genius is the birthright of every normal individual." Alas! we have all tried many times to hoist ourselves by our own suspenders, as the Americans say, and have found that it cannot be done!

But George Herbert reminds us that "who aimeth at the sky shoots higher much than he that means a tree," and Robert Burns that "who does the utmost that he can will whiles do mair." By aiming at genius we may achieve a more respectable mediocrity.

The writer thinks that because we are so slack about becoming our own masters, we are being enslaved to machinery and dictatorship. Already, he says, over more than half Europe the familiar landmarks are being submerged; truth and culture, liberty and justice, are dishonoured memories: tyranny and violence have achieved what seems to be a final victory over all that civilized man has held for good.

I do not agree that it is a final victory; revolutions do not change human nature. As Menander says, "You cannot straighten a crooked branch; no one can force necessity or nature." For better and for worse, the pendulum will swing back.

But it is true that we are becoming dangerously machine-minded. The savage can build his own house in a day. We need machines for mowing a lawn, sweeping a room, and toasting a piece of bread. "You press the button, we do the rest," is the motto of modern civilization.

The real subject of the book is "The Mass Production of Robots." We are not free men. We have to think as the herd thinks, that we may be driven as the herd is driven. We must feel as the herd feels, bellow as it bellows, charge and trample or be trampled on in unison with the mob.

Mind, soul and conscience have died to be reborn into the mass egoism of nation, party or class. Man is no longer a living soul, but a cog in a standardized machine. He has no rights and no claims to personal dignity; it is characteristic of the totalitarian mentality that it finds a holy delight in crushing and humiliating anyone suspected of independence.

The whole community, in Russia, Germany and Italy, is worked up into a state of violent collective excitement. They must yell for hours on end, "Great is Diana of the Ephesians," or words to that effect, and they must foam at the mouth, to order, against some selected enemy.

The technique of tyranny, of making a government omnipotent, has been carried to far greater perfection in the last twenty years than ever before. Modern inventions have made despotism much more searching than the most ferocious autocracies of past history. This, and not any particular form of government—Communist or anti-Communist— is the important and sinister discovery of post-war Europe.

Fülöp Miller compared the methods of Bolshevism to those of the Jesuits, and Wingfield-Stratford draws the same parallel. The rulers are an order of initiates, carefully chosen and frequently purged, who have sacrificed all their individuality, and obey "like a dead corpse," as Ignatius of Loyola said. The method is horribly effective, and it has been reinforced by the resources of modern science.

The new science of suggestion aims at turning out human units in the mass, like the products of factories. It is equipped with resources such as Nero and Torquemada never dreamed of. "It will soon be possible for the same Satan to whisper the same suggestion into the ears of every Eve and every Adam from China to Peru, and, by television, to appear before them in any form he chooses. It is a task of the utmost simplicity to prevent them from hearing or seeing anything else bearing on the subject—most of all, the truth."

Sir Walter Citrine, an orthodox trade unionist who has just come back from Russia, is appalled by the thoroughness of the technique of State socialism.

This is the method. "Get hold of the children in the crêche. Follow them through the kindergarten, then through the school. Then get them into the Pioneers or the young Komsomols. Keep at them with incessant propaganda. Propaganda! propaganda! from morning to night. On the wireless, films, pictures, posters, follow them everywhere. Mussolini and Hitler have done the same; they, too, move in public amid cheering crowds. But this new technique of repression and propaganda, where will it all end?"

I have no space for Wingfield-Stratford's rules of training, which are sensible enough. He speaks of an odious little book called *Filling up the Chinks*, which was given him when he was a child. We are not to be always stuffing our minds with useful information.

"Reading makes a full man," says Bacon. Yes, but the full man suffers horribly from indigestion.

Nevertheless, I think he is too hard on time-killing devices for hours of idleness. Perhaps we ought to spend our leisure hours in voyaging through strange seas of thought alone, like Newton; but the fact is that we often want to escape from our own company.

It is strange, but true, that I have known a Prime Minister who spent hours a day playing bridge, two eminent scholars who digested their dinners with the help of crossword puzzles, and one would-be philosopher (myself) who has been known to take a detective novel to read on a long journey.

To return to our robots. The danger is great. There is no law of nature by which the countrymen of Shakespeare and Milton are exempt from the fate which has overtaken those of Leonardo, Goethe, and Tolstóy.

The only safeguard is that there shall be a large number of people who are both able and willing to maintain their personal independence, to say what they think, to do what they know to be right, and to refuse to prostitute their minds, their pens, and their votes.

There are many whom we can hardly ask to resist the machine which enslaves them. It would not be becoming in me, who am unusually free, to blame the less fortunate. But under a totalitarian State there would be *nobody* who could speak and act freely, except at the price of instant martyrdom. This is what Herbert Spencer meant when he said that State-socialism (or State-capitalism) means slavery, and that the slavery would not be mild.

Some self-sacrifice is demanded, even now. It

can be expected only from those who have strong religious convictions—using religion for any resolve "because right is right to follow right in scorn of consequence."

The best way of getting "new minds for old" is to follow Christ. Those who have not this happiness may at least remember the noble words of Spinoza, after whom the Nazi Government will no longer allow streets to be named. "Love for the eternal and infinite feeds the mind with pure delight, and is wholly free from every taint of sorrow; herein must lie the supreme goal of our desire, to be sought with all our strength."

This is the secret of perfect freedom. "Good or bad character (*mores*)," says Augustine, "depends on good or bad loves (*amores*)."

Such a man is the Lord's servant, the world's master, and his own man.

VIII

WORK AND PLAY

I

THE last volume of the *New Survey of London Life and Labour* is very interesting. It is called *Life and Leisure*, and contains a well-informed and sympathetic study of how the modern Londoner spends his time when he is not at work.

If it is true that "all the forces are combining to shift the main centre of a worker's life more and more from his daily work to his daily leisure," we cannot deny the great importance of such a study as this.

The first thing that struck me in reading the book was that if we spoke to a working man, as we are in the habit of speaking among ourselves, of the happy old times before the war, he would disagree with us emphatically. He is much better off now than he was twenty-five years ago.

No part of the terrific war debt of eight or ten thousand million pounds has been laid on his shoulders. The landed gentry have been practically wiped out by taxation; the professional and upper middle class have had to reduce their standard of living in a drastic manner; there are a hundred thousand fewer maidservants in London than there were a generation ago.

But the London worker's daily labour is shorter by about an hour, and whereas in Charles Booth's survey only two-thirds of the population were above the poverty-line, we now read with surprise that "in 1930 the average London working-class family had a margin of income above minimum physical needs amounting to thirty-four shillings and sixpence in a week of full employment."

It seems certain that so far as creature-comforts and opportunities for enjoyment are concerned, there never has been a time when life was so good for the common man as it is in England to-day. Still further improvements may be possible; but bitter discontent is surely out of place. Have we not heard enough of "wage-slaves"?

How do the masses spend their leisure? As compared with forty years ago they have a much greater variety of amusements, and women and girls now have, as they had not then, almost as many facilities for enjoying themselves as the men.

Moving pictures were beginning to come in at the beginning of the century; at present the cinema is *par excellence* the people's amusement. The seating accommodation in some 250 cinemas is nearly 350,000.

The popularity of the music-hall has declined. Perhaps the wireless set, which is now to be seen everywhere in working-class homes, is even more important as a social influence than the cinema. It is, I think, by far the finest educational instrument ever brought within the reach of the masses, and I cannot help hoping that it may promote more sympathy and better understanding among the nations of Europe.

Watching games is an extremely popular way of spending time. The attendance at Football Cup Finals has lately exceeded 90,000. As for the new sport of greyhound racing, the total attendances in 1932 exceeded nine million. Motor-cycle races attract about 1,300,000 spectators a year. Cricket may have reached its zenith from the point of view of the spectator, and lawn-tennis, though perhaps the best of all games to watch, is also one of the most expensive. Boxing, to judge from the newspapers, excites keen interest.

Dancing, swimming, and walking have increased greatly in popularity since the war, and seem to attract all classes equally. The appreciation of good music is certainly more widely spread than it was forty years ago.

The holiday habit is now almost universal. A modern Mr. and Mrs. Gilpin, who have had no holiday in "twice ten tedious years," would now be impossible to find. A week or more at the seaside seems to be the favourite outing, but a surprising number manage to cross the Channel to France or Belgium.

Our authorities estimate the average cost of a week's holiday in August at not less than ten pounds per family—a large item in the yearly budget.

These are the recreations of a pleasure-loving, sociable, good-humoured, civilized people, fundamentally sound at heart.

The more intellectual pleasures attract as many as we have a right to expect. Those who have had what are considered the highest educational advantages are not always eager to use them!

In England it seems almost an insult to point out that the populace have no taste either for indecency or for cruelty. But it is not so in all civilized countries, nor has it always been so in our own.

The writers call the third part of their survey "Indulgence and Delinquency," but they are not at all censorious.

The working man does not admit that there is any longer a drink question in England, and the statistics of the consumption of alcohol show that on an average he is very temperate. The consumption of beer has declined from 46 standard gallons a head in 1891 to 23 in 1928, and the beer is not so strong as it was. A pint and a half a day for each man, and half a pint for his wife, cannot be called excessive, and this seems to be about the average. On the other hand, it is a rather large item in the working family's budget. If I had to bring up a family on £200 a year I should not spend 15 per cent of it on alcoholic drinks. The consumption of spirits is happily on the decline.

This is not the place to discuss sexual irregularities, to which the authors allot a good deal of space. The most remarkable fact is that prostitution is actually dying out. St. Augustine thought that such a reform was quite impossible, and until lately almost everyone would have agreed with him.

The chapter on crime I find unsatisfactory. What is the use of counting up the convictions for burglary? We want to know the sum-total of robberies, which it seems to me are becoming disgracefully frequent.

I do not think the authors are severe enough upon betting and gambling, which is unquestionably our chief national vice at present. The writer of the chapter on this subject does not see that betting is wrong, and the worst of it is that most people agree with him. As long as public opinion does not condemn the practice, it is useless to try to legislate against it. It is a vice of the aristocracy and the populace. The middle class, of course with numerous exceptions, do not bet or gamble; but the time is past when that estimable section of the nation could impose its will on the others. That patient ass, bowed between two burdens, has to pay the piper, but he is not allowed to call the tune. The clergy can denounce betting from the pulpit; but those who need their exhortations are not there to listen to them.

I have left myself no space for what I chiefly wanted to discuss—the change in opinion about the supreme value of industry and hard work. It

is one of the most interesting changes in our time,
and is likely to have very important consequences.
But I must hold over my remarks upon it till the
next chapter, except for this little story.

A rich man, in Abraham's bosom as he supposed, becoming terribly bored, asked an angel to
find him some work to do.

"Sorry, sir, it is impossible."

"Well, I think it very odd that in heaven such
a reasonable request should be refused."

"My good man, you are not in heaven."

VIII—*continued*

WORK AND PLAY

II

"It is commonly believed that happiness consists
in leisure. We forgo leisure in order that we may
have leisure, just as we go to war in order that we
may have peace."

This quotation is from Aristotle. The illustration
is perhaps unfortunate. Every war is said to be
"a war to end war," and every war only begets
other wars. So we work in order to provide for
our old age; but the work-habit ends by making
leisure intolerable.

Bernard Shaw, who, in spite of his revolutionary
ideas, is an old Victorian, like myself, says that
the essence of hell is a perpetual holiday.

But, to do Aristotle justice, when he says leisure
he does not mean idleness. Happiness for him is
"an activity of the soul in a complete life"; he
distinguishes leisure not only from work but from
play. Leisure includes all the things that we do for
their own sakes—the pursuit of real as opposed to
merely instrumental values. We have borrowed his
word for leisure, but we pronounce it "school."

Carlyle, however, preached a gospel of work for
work's sake; it is one of his favourite themes. He

was shocked that the sentence upon Adam, "In the sweat of thy face thou shalt eat bread," should be regarded as a curse, and not a blessing.

We shall not find this glorification of work for its own sake much before Calvin. He taught that hard work is the best form of self-discipline. This teaching has had an immense effect upon modern civilization.

The modern business man, if he is not a child of the Ghetto, is generally a grandchild of John Calvin. The nations where his discipline has prevailed have become very rich, but they have too often forgotten that money is only an instrument for a reasonable and beautiful life; Calvinistic civilization has not been either intelligent or beautiful.

For better or worse, the gospel of work is now discredited. Many good reasons might be found for this, but the chief reason is that it is no longer blessed by the economists. Carlyle's cry, "Produce! Produce! If it is only a fraction of a product, produce it in heaven's name!" seems to rest on an economic fallacy. In an age of machinery the world can produce much more than it can use.

The American remedy was what was called "consumptionism." Multiply wants, persuade everybody to buy (mostly on credit) a number of things which they do not need; and so keep business humming. It did hum for a good many years; then it rather suddenly stopped.

Another plan is to reduce the day's work from eight hours to four, and to pay the workmen as much for half a day as for the whole. This sounds like an excellent plan—for a general election. At other times it is hardly worth discussing; and what a miserable prospect, to be allowed to work for only four hours a day!

It seems to me that one of the most important questions is this: Ought we to distinguish sharply a man's work from his leisure? Ought we to acquiesce in the servile tradition that a man only works because he is obliged; that he naturally hates his work and wants to escape from it; that he cannot be expected to take any interest in it; that he only begins to *live* when a bell rings and releases him?

This seems to me a wretched view of life. The truly happy man is surely the man whose work is his play, and his play merely recreation. "The finest kinds of work and the finest kinds of play," says Dr. L. P. Jacks, "are almost indistinguishable; it is only on their lower levels that work and play are opposites." I have certainly found it so myself.

Am I working or playing at this moment? I do not know. I enjoy thinking and reading and writing, and, since I am not a practical organizer, I think this is the best use I can make of the moderate abilities with which I have been endowed. If I had to knock off after four hours I should be miserable.

It is often said that the mechanization of labour makes it so dull that the workman cannot enjoy his work, while the constant repetition of the same manual motions is irritating to the nerves. There is undoubtedly some truth in this.

The most enjoyable kind of work is artistic production; and what is to become of the poor artist when drawing, painting, modelling and designing, music, acting and other gifts of the Muses, are produced by machinery? Nevertheless, there are two sources of boredom which I believe to be more important. The first is working in a bad spirit, a disloyal, grudging temper.

Such success as the Russian Communists have had, in spite of their monstrous cruelty and tyranny, is due to the enthusiasm which they have been able to create in many of their workmen. When the team-spirit is raised to fever-heat there is no more boredom, but a keen pleasure in doing one's best.

The other source should appeal to the conscience of the consumer. "What is the use of talking to me about the dignity of labour?" said a working man to Dr. Jacks. "What is the use of preaching about my duties to the public when I know that the public I am working for are a lot of d——d fools?"

If the consumer realized that he has no right to degrade humanity by obliging a man to make things which had better not be made, or to waste another man's life in ministering only to silly amusement and vulgar ostentation, I believe there would be far less discontent among the workers, and I honour a man for being discontented in such circumstances.

The four-hours working day is nonsense; but the workman in the future is likely to have more than half his waking hours at his own disposal. Can we train ourselves and each other in the use of leisure?

The *New Survey of London Life*, which suggested these two articles to me, does justice to the many admirable organizations which already try to meet this need. But Dr. Jacks, in the American lectures to which I have referred, thinks that something more is needed to satisfy the "skill-hunger," the creative instinct, which is dormant in every normal man. While this is unsatisfied he cannot be happy. If the conditions of mechanized production prevent this instinct from being satisfied in working hours, there ought to be readily accessible institutions for teaching all the arts and crafts, not for commerce, but as serious and delightful hobbies.

He says that a National Recreation School already exists in New York, and a College of Recreational Culture in Sweden, a country which has taken the lead in excellent educational experiments. This suggestion seems well worth consideration.

I cannot refrain from quoting a passage from Ecclesiasticus on "the dignity of labour"; I think it is unique at the time it was written. The writer is no democrat. "The artificers," he says, "shall not be sought for in the council of the people; wisdom cometh by opportunity of leisure." (This is the Greek doctrine.) *"But they maintain the fabric of the world, and in the handiwork of their craft is their prayer."*

Is not this a fine saying?

IX

PRIVATE VICES, PUBLIC BENEFITS

THE *Fable of the Bees; or, Private Vices, Public Benefits* made a first-class scandal in the reign of George I. It was the work of Bernard Mandeville, by birth a Dutchman, and a rather obscure doctor—at least, the Royal College of Physicians took no notice of him. Nor did the public take much notice of his poem when it first appeared in 1705, nor when it was expanded in prose in 1714.

But the second edition, in 1723, produced an explosion of outraged virtue. The Grand Jury of Middlesex "presented" the book, and ordered it to be burnt by the public hangman, which of course gave it a splendid advertisement. It was still easy to acquire, and everybody bought it. The heaviest guns were brought to bear upon it. Bishop Berkeley the philosopher, William Law the divine, and Adam Smith the economist all wrote refutations.

It was not worth while to break a butterfly on the wheel, and Mandeville was only half serious. He was annoyed by the contemporary optimists—optimists are very irritating people—who argued that society is founded on the virtues of mankind. So he propounded the startling thesis that "those who will give themselves leisure to gaze on the prospect of concatenated events may in a hundred places see good spring up and pullulate from evil, as naturally as chickens do from eggs."

Berkeley summarizes, and hardly parodies, the argument. Take each particular vice and trace it through its consequences, and you will clearly perceive the advantage it brings to the public.

Drunkenness, for instance, increases the malt tax, a principal branch of His Majesty's revenue, and thereby promotes the safety, strength and glory of the nation. Secondly, it employs a great number of hands, farmers, brewers, innkeepers and others. "Your half-witted folk censure gaming," which employs cardmakers and others. "Poverty is relieved, ingenuity rewarded, and the money has a lively circulation."

Most of Berkeley's indignation is directed against the economic fallacy which John Stuart Mill thought he had killed—the notion that it is good for trade to squander money unproductively. There is an amusing skit on this fallacy, beginning:

> Now Dives daily feasted and was gorgeously arrayed,
> Not at all because he liked it, but because 'twas
> good for trade.

But it is not dead by any means. One hears it every day. Multiply wants and gratify them freely; spend all you can, and keep money in rapid circulation. Then everyone profits, and trade hums. This was honoured both in theory and practice till the great slump in 1929, but I do not think the old-fashioned virtue of thrift is held in much honour even now. Some of our economists have thrown over Mill and his theories, and exhort us to spend instead of saving.

Mandeville will not find a champion in me. So far is it from being true that private vices are public benefits, every bad man is a centre of demoralization, and different vices often combine to make terrible crimes possible.

What the New Testament calls "the world" is a system of co-operative guilt with limited liability. The Crucifixion was possible only by the co-operation of a cowardly governor, unscrupulous ecclesiastics, a traitor disciple, a thoughtless mob, and callous executioners. None of them was bad enough to carry through the whole crime alone. Happily, the ramifications of goodness are also far-reaching, though they are less easy to trace.

In a lighter vein, we might defend a corollary to Mandeville's thesis, and maintain that private virtues are often public nuisances.

It has been said cynically that the wise are occupied in trying to undo the mischief wrought by the good. Humanitarian sentiment is often kind only to be cruel. William Law, who was so indignant with Mandeville, used to let canaries out of cages, no doubt to fall a prey to the nearest cat; and the parish where he lived was a happy hunting-ground of fraudulent beggars. There was once a canon of St. Paul's who scattered half-crowns on the way from Amen Court to the cathedral. The result may be imagined.

Butthe most obvious example of my maxim, which must not be accepted too seriously, is the tiresome class of people who think that "because they are virtuous, there shall be no more cakes and ale." They flourish like a green bay tree in America, and at home wherever the owners of a Nonconformist conscience meet together.

I happened to visit America during the unsuccessful attempt to enforce Prohibition. Sermons against "booze" were advertised everywhere, generally delivered by a perspiring fanatic, who would demonstrate his love of temperance by smashing a chair or two on the platform.

Before I landed, I was of course asked by a group of reporters what I thought of Prohibition. I replied that I had no objection to observe the law for three weeks; but "since you ask me," I added, "I think that cold water, with which, as the Psalmist says, the wild asses quench their thirst, is a poor beverage to offer to a human being." In reality, I was quite content, like Thackeray's Valoroso, to "quaff no other fount than nature's rill."

Private virtues, founded on ignorance and stupidity, are really public nuisances. An unenlightened conscience is a peculiarly dangerous obstacle to reform.

Sometimes the whole nation is swept by a storm

of virtuous indignation, as was the case last year about Italy and Abyssinia. In this instance, I fully shared the indignation; but it must be admitted that Sir Samuel Hoare and M. Laval tried to get much better terms for the unhappy Abyssinians than they ultimately obtained.

To do evil that good may come can never be right. The doctrine that national crimes may be public benefits may yet bring our civilization to ruin.

X

TALKING

In what company is one likely to hear the best conversation?

I should say, among lawyers. A guest-night at the Temple or Lincoln's Inn is always a treat. They have two excellent rules. They print on their cards of invitation, "No music; no speeches." These two methods of barbarism, which make most banquets so irritating and wearisome, have been abolished. And they rearrange the company for dessert, so that one is not tied to the same neighbours for the whole evening. The talk is also uniformly good.

Business men I find less interesting, though I agree with Dr. Johnson that a man is seldom more innocently employed than when he is making money.

I like talking to medical men, and the High Table of an Oxford or Cambridge college is often very pleasant, though one is occasionally reminded of Mark Twain's story of the man who had a million-pound bank-note in his pocket, and no small change.

The complaint is often made that the parochial clergy are rather dull. If it is true, I think the reason is that laymen will not talk freely to them. I noticed the difference at once when I first put on clerical dress.

Some people say that the Irish are better talkers than the English. I have no doubt that the Irish peasant is wittier and more voluble than the corresponding class in England; but an Irishman's conversation is apt to fall into premature anecdotage, which is not the best kind of talk.

As for the Scotch, there is a grain of truth in Charles Lamb's complaint of their matter-of-factness; but they are very good company for all that.

The proverbs of all nations warn us that the tongue is a dangerous organ. "Speech is silver, silence is gold." "He who knows not how to be silent knows not how to speak."

> If you your lips will keep from slips,
>   Five things observe with care,
> Of whom you speak, to whom you speak,
>   And how and when and where.

Benjamin Franklin, however, protests that if we must give account for every idle word, so we must for every idle silence. This is no doubt true; but conversation ought to be intermittent, not continuous. The non-stop talker is a terrible bore. I have heard of a mischievous hostess who invited two tremendous talkers to meet each other at dinner. Both of them passed the soup for fear that his rival might get going during the first course.

The epitaph on these athletes of the tongue ought to be not "*hic jacet*," but "*hic tacet*."

Professor Pearl, of Baltimore, showed me an experiment which he had made with rats. The male rat is very stationary; the female may cover twenty miles a night. If there were a machine for measuring loquacity, it would probably be found that women speak ten times as many words as men.

We know that in some religious orders long silences are prescribed. The Trappists, I believe, sometimes take vows of perpetual dumbness. Have there ever been any female Trappists? I doubt it; the penance would be too cruel.

If this sounds impolite, I hasten to add that though many women have always been delightful to listen to, their conversation seems to me to be more interesting than it was in Queen Victoria's reign. They have more interests and there are not so many troublesome taboos.

Some of the most eloquent advocates of taciturnity have been by no means reluctant to give their opinions to the world. Carlyle sang the praises of silence in about thirty-seven octavo volumes. He is partly responsible for the cult of the strong, silent man.

There have, I admit, been a few strong, silent men. Moltke was one of those who were said to be "silent in seven languages." He was not easily moved to display any emotion. There were only two occasions when he was seen to laugh—one when he heard of his mother-in-law's death, and the other when someone told him that the Swedes considered Stockholm a fortress.

It is said, probably truly, that the most brilliant conversation ever heard was that of the idle French aristocracy of the eighteenth century, in the salons of Paris. The French have always cultivated talking as a fine art; even Julius Caesar says that the Gauls value most highly "fighting and clever conversation." So it is not surprising that we find in La Rochefoucauld some shrewd hints about what to avoid in conversing: "Our self-love suffers with more impatience the condemnation of our tastes than of our opinions." "In conversation the worst blunder is to try to please oneself rather than the other party." "We can pardon those who bore us, but not those whom we bore." "Nothing hinders us from being natural so much as the wish to appear so." "We talk spitefully more from vanity than from malice."

I think, however, that it is not so much vanity as the wish to say something interesting that makes us retail gossip. We think that one touch of ill-nature makes the whole world kin. And the same motive makes us repeat bits of information which it would have been more discreet to keep to ourselves.

"Sir, you have only two subjects, yourself and myself, and I am sick of both," said Dr. Johnson to an unlucky fellow who was trying to please him.

Educated people certainly try to talk of things

rather than persons; but here there is a danger of becoming controversial. The most important subjects, such as religion and politics, are just those on which people lose their tempers, and which in consequence we avoid unless we know that the person to whom we are speaking thinks as we do.

The pleasantest talks are between two friends who know and like each other well. They ramble on without effort on either side. Ideas are exchanged and sympathies strengthened.

The great talkers cannot expect to be remembered after they are dead.

What would Socrates be to us without Plato, or Johnson without Boswell? Coleridge's *Table Talk* makes good reading, but it is hardly conversation, for he seems to have done all the talking himself.

"I think, Charles, that you never heard me preach," he said to Lamb.

"My dear boy," replied Lamb, "I never heard you do anything else."

POLITICAL

I

DEMOCRACY ON THE DEFENSIVE

I HAVE been reading Mr. Delisle Burns on *Democracy* in the Home University Library. There is a pleasant Victorian flavour about it, as there is in all pleas for democracy. Even our dusty, fusty, musty old friend, "Force is no remedy," is brought out of the cupboard. If I find a burglar in my house, am I to take up a poker? Oh, no! I am to *persuade him to go*. Democracy—*c'est la paix*. This was not at all the opinion of Lord Salisbury, who knew something of foreign politics.

Democracy, says Mr. Burns, is a word with many meanings and some emotional colour. It is indeed. When I was in America I culled two gems from the newspapers. The first was by a divinity professor: "You cannot separate God and Democracy. For if we believe in God, we believe in God's purposes, God's ideal." The minor premiss that Democracy is God's ideal, was, I suppose, too obvious to need stating. The second was medical. "Uric acid is tottering on its throne. Democracy is advancing in medical theory as well as in political practice."

I hardly expected to find this religious enthusiasm for a word which after all means only an experiment in government, on this side of the Atlantic. But Mr. Burns is almost equally lyrical. "The principles of science are the principles of Democracy," which must therefore have the credit for all modern inventions.

It is like some old-fashioned books of apologetics, in which all progress is put down to Christianity. In reality, science, like history, is a good aristocrat, and democracy is always obscurantist. Universal suffrage would have restored the Stuarts and prevented the reform of the calendar. It would have prohibited the power-loom and spinning-jenny and vaccination. It is capable of voting that the earth is flat, that Darwin was a fool (as in Tennessee), and that the English are the lost Ten Tribes.

Hitler in Germany, and (to give the devil his due) Stalin in Russia, have introduced some really scientific legislation such as we shall never see in England while we keep our present system of government.

Democracy, Mr. Burns says, proceeds on the assumption that all men are equal, in order to discover who are the best.

To start with an assumption which, as Carlyle says, is "a palpable incredibility and a delirious absurdity," is an odd way of arriving at desirable results. But Mr. Burns thinks that those who speak thus dislike democracy only "because it does not permit *them* to rule." "The nature of man is such that not even a successful dramatist" (that means Mr. G. B. Shaw) "nor a dean" (that means me) "could maintain his excellence if he were a dictator."

I am not aware that either Mr. Shaw or I have ever wished to be a dictator. If the power was shared between us, like the Roman consuls, the results would certainly be curious.

Modern democracy, as the author says, is a very new experiment. We cannot compare the Athenian or Roman republics, which were slave-states. And the founders of the American republic really wanted democracy for good aristocrats, as Luther and Henry VIII wanted Protestantism for good Catholics. It is a very new experiment, and it does not seem likely to last long. The German publicist, von Sybel, long ago predicted that universal suffrage would sound the knell of popular government.

The reasons for this are plain, and were given admirably by Plato. At first democracy means the abolition of privileges, and freedom for everybody to do as he likes. "Even the domestic animals strut about proudly." But it soon degenerates into an auction of the worldly goods of the minority. Government becomes more and more extravagant and rapacious, till the nation bleeds to death. And then the way is open for a dictator, for when a steam-roller has been driven over a nation, levelling all distinctions, the power of resistance to despotism is very small. I think history has proved this up to the hilt. Mr. Burns would like the steam-

231

roller. But why is he so fond of a Dutch landscape, all as flat as a pancake? Would it really be a pleasant country to live in?

Quite consistently he wants to abolish all schools except those provided by the State. The public schools are, as he says, the custodians of certain traditions, and he does not like the traditions. That is a matter of opinion; but would it be a good thing to turn out everybody alike? Would it even be a good thing to do away with all the prizes in a lottery where there must always be so many blanks? Human beings, at least in this country, like a little adventure; they are not averse to gambling, the essence of which is the chance of winning money that you have not earned. The poor wish to fleece the rich, of course, now that they have the chance—and it may often be good for the soul's health of the rich to be plundered—but our people are not enamoured of equality, and are not displeased that the lucky ones should behave as they would like to behave themselves. Envy and hatred—almost the only sins to which no pleasure is attached—are not so strong in England as our revolutionists would like them to be.

The new snobbery, so much more servile and obsequious than the old, places "the upper classes" between deprecating inverted commas. We shall soon have people giving their address apologetically as "Upper" Tooting or "High" Wycombe. It is a pity that nowadays, when the gentleman never remembers his class, some others are never able to forget it.

There is, however, a great deal that is good in this book. If "Democracy" can be extended to mean a form of *society* rather than a form of government, I for one am in favour of it. "Treat humanity always as an end, never as a means." This maxim of Kant is thoroughly Christian.

Also, Mr. Burns's indictment of the new dictatorships is unanswerable. He shows that they are the aftermath of the Great War, and hopes that they will not last long. But will Russia, or Italy, or Germany, or Turkey wish to substitute for tyranny his beloved democracy? That seems very doubtful indeed. Its inventors, France and England, are none too well satisfied with the way it works.

Personally, I should be very sorry to live under a dictatorship, for I like to say what I think. In Italy I should be dosed with castor-oil and banished to the Lipari Islands; in Germany I should be beaten and put into a concentration camp. In Russia I should be lucky if I were only shot.

Helvétius wrote to Montesquieu: "I have never understood the subtle distinctions between different kinds of government. I only know of two, the good and the bad. The good has never yet existed; the bad consists of transferring, on one pretext or another, the property of the governed to the pockets of the governors."

If this is true, and it is, what ought the helpless

233

intelligentsia to do? Not to float with the stream, a feat which any dead dog can accomplish. Not to lick the boots of our masters, a complaisance which any live dog is willing to render. Let us keep our self-respect, if we can keep nothing else, and leave others to be court chaplains to King Demos.

II

PEOPLE OUR EMPIRE

A few months ago Commissioner Lamb, of the
Salvation Army, wrote: "This country has during
the last decade spent over a thousand millions on
the relief of able-bodied men and women, and got
nothing for it but a heritage of misery and demoralization. Could it not well risk a like sum in endea-
vours to establish communities which give promise
of ultimately becoming self-supporting?"

The distribution of population in various parts
of the globe is grotesque. The average density,
excluding the uninhabitable regions, is about
thirty-six per square mile. England has eight
hundred per square mile, Belgium six hundred and
sixty-four, Holland five hundred and fifty-four,
Italy three hundred and sixty, the United States
thirty-eight, the Argentine Republic eight, Canada
three, Australia two.

Premier Hughes of Australia thought that his
country might well support a hundred million
people. Of course I know that part of Australia
is desert, and part of Canada too cold to live in;
but it would be a very moderate estimate to say
that both countries could find room for eight times
their present population.

New Zealand, too, which its former Governor,

Lord Bledisloe, has described as an earthly paradise, has a population of under two millions and an area only slightly less than that of the British Isles.

These three empty countries are all under our flag; those who settle in them are an asset to the British Commonwealth of Nations.

The results of overcrowding at home are seen not only in the presence of two millions permanently unemployed. People will not have children when there is obviously no room for them. In 1881 the population of England and Wales was twenty-six millions, the births nine hundred thousand. In 1931 the population was forty millions, the births six hundred and thirty thousand. To every thousand persons in England and Wales fifty years ago there were thirty-four births; to-day there are fourteen or fifteen.

A comparison with other nations will show what is happening to us. In 1930 the annual excess of births was five per thousand in the United Kingdom, twelve in Italy, seventeen in Poland, and twenty-four in European Russia, if the Soviet statistics are reliable.

I do not mean to suggest that nothing has been done. In 1922, under the Empire Settlement Act, three million pounds was made available every year for fifteen years to secure a better distribution of the Empire; but of the forty millions available only seven millions have been spent.

The Canadian Immigration Department distri-

236

butes pamphlets and text-books by the hundred thousand. Australia is, or was till the recent slump, willing to receive and to assist a large number of selected immigrants. I fear things are not made too easy for them now.

In fact, emigration is now almost non-existent; those who leave our shores hardly balance those who come in. Australians themselves speak bitterly of the selfish and short-sighted policy of the Labour Party in their country, and no doubt care must be taken to dispel any suspicion that the newcomers are intended to compete in the labour market with those already in Australia.

But I believe that this can be done, and well-instructed opinion in the Commonwealth realizes the danger of a dog-in-the-manger attitude towards immigration. If the white man is kept out the yellow man may force his way in.

What I complain of is that there is no steam behind the movement in this country. The congestion of population is the most important question tion before us—perhaps a matter of life and death for our nation; and our Government cares nothing about it; it plumes itself on building houses to help people to marry on the dole, but as for finding a real remedy for unemployment, nothing is done.

We are sometimes told that our people will not go and cannot be made to go. They are afraid of finding themselves out of work in countries where the provision for the unemployed is less generous than it is here. It is also said that we no longer breed good emigrants.

I am naturally unable to deal with these objections at first hand; but Commissioner Lamb is well qualified to judge, and he is confident that they are untrue. "In 1928," he says, "the Industrial Transference Board reported that there was in this country an abundance of first-class material, and the Dominions Secretary has told us repeatedly that for years past there has never been less than fifty thousand people willing to go overseas."

I hope there are many more. The Australians say that one difficulty is that almost all Englishmen have acquired "the wage-habit." They prefer to work for fixed sums and to take no risks. But this difficulty is not insuperable.

I am strongly in favour of group settlement in the place of individual infiltration. There must be large areas of unoccupied good land in West Australia, in New Zealand, in Tasmania, and probably in other places.

My idea is that our Government should buy large areas in half-empty countries, and settle upon them carefully selected groups which would constitute self-contained and, before long, self-supporting communities.

These new communities would not interfere with the labour market in the great towns; they would add to the wealth of the country, and each of them would provide a happy and useful existence for many thousands of our countrymen.

I suggest that these groups should be drawn as far as possible from the same districts. Each county should interest itself in some one group, and the new town might be called Bedford or Exeter or Durham, or whatever district the inhabitants came from. The settlement would then be fed, as opportunities arose, with fresh emigrants from the same county, and in some cases the mother-county might help its child by buying the surplus produce of the new community.

The next fifty years will decide for all future time whether our race is to remain one of the great peoples of the world, or whether we shall throw away the most amazing of good fortunes, and most splendid of opportunities, ever offered to any nation. History will judge us.

Fifty years hence there will be no more empty countries. The British Empire will be inhabited either by our own people or by aliens. We are dropping behind in the race, though we had a long start. We did not lose North America in the reign of George III; but we are losing it now: the Anglo-Saxon element in the population is being swamped.

So it may be in Canada, Australasia, and South Africa. Sir John Seeley said that we conquered half the world in a fit of absence of mind. It looks as if we meant to lose it in a fit of absence of mind. The twentieth century will decide; we shall never have another chance.

III

JEW-BAITING

I USED to think that Jew-baiting was more or less a fad of Hitler's own or at any rate a new craze since the Russian revolution, in which some of the leaders, such as Trotsky and Zinovieff, were Jews. I was mistaken.

In that fascinating book, recently published, *John Bailey's Letters and Diaries*, packed with good stories and brilliant sayings from end to end, the following note appears, written in 1915:

> *"Grey told Kitchener that the last time he ever saw the Kaiser, at a luncheon party, he [the Kaiser] began abusing the Jews to him, and when Grey tried to calm him down and told him that we managed very well with our Jews in England, he replied, hissing with hatred, 'I tell you, Sir Edward, what ought to be done with the German Jews; they ought to be killed, killed, killed!'"*

When I have talked to Germans, they have only said that many Jews are Communists.

But a friend of mine, who has a Scottish wife, told me that Hitler himself said to him, in reply to a remonstrance: "What would the Scotch think if three-quarters of the good posts at Edinburgh were held, I won't say by Jews, but by Englishmen?"

240

To which, of course, the answer is that the Scotch take very good care that not even one-quarter of any posts worth having shall be held by Englishmen.

The Germans have the reputation of being a tough and hard-working race; are they really unable to hold their own against the Jews without violence?

Perhaps the Jews are not exactly popular anywhere, but Englishmen are always indignant at manifest injustice, and I hope always will be.

The only people in England who were not shocked at the persecution of poor Captain Dreyfus were Mr. Belloc and perhaps the schoolboy who translated "Le jeu ne vaut pas la chandelle" by "The Jew is not worth the scandal"; this, he explained quite correctly, is what the French are saying. The systematic persecution of the German Jews has not even this pitiful excuse. It fills us with stupefaction. Are we in the twentieth century, or back in the Dark Ages?

Anyone who reads the Pentateuch carefully must see that Moses was determined, if possible, to prevent the Hebrews from doing what during the greater part of their history they have done. He wished them to remain a simple pastoral people, a tribe of Bedouins. This became impossible, and I do not think we can blame the Jews of the Dispersion if they were driven to money-lending.

Q

There were few other occupations from which they were not debarred.

The Jews seem to have been always unpopular. The terse historian Tacitus, who never wastes a word, says that the Emperor Tiberius banished four thousand of them to Sardinia—"A cheap loss (*vile damnum*) if they died from the unhealthiness of the climate."

Our King Edward I banished all Jews from England—in order, so the Jews said, to make way for "the Papal merchants and the Pope's usurers, who have supplanted us."

The Spanish Inquisition was very busy with the burning of Jews in large batches. These shows were at once religious ceremonies and public amusements. There is, or used to be, according to Lecky, a picture at Madrid representing a procession to the stake of a number of Jews and Jewesses in 1680, on the occasion of the King's marriage. The King and Queen are looking on.

St. Louis of France, when asked how a Jewish controversialist should be answered, replied: "The best answer a layman can make to a contumacious Jew is to run his sword into him as far as it will go."

Nearly all the recent laws in Germany against the Jews are revivals of laws passed in the Middle Ages, when the Jews were obliged to wear a distinctive dress and to live in separate parts of the towns.

A Christian then might not enter into partnership with them; they might not use the public baths;

they might not be physicians, surgeons or chemists. Inter-marriage was forbidden, and a Christian who took a Jewess for his mistress might be burned alive. A Jew who entered a Christian (!) disorderly house was severely punished.

To us this kind of thing is simply unintelligible. Most of us have Jews among our friends, and find them very much like Christians. We have no objection to making a Jew Prime Minister or Viceroy of India, if we think he is the best man for the job. Disraeli made Jews his heroes in some of his novels, and we liked him the better for it.

In the Middle Ages, religious fanaticism was at the bottom of the persecutions; the priests and monks hounded on the government and the populace. In 1390 four thousand Jews were massacred at Seville at the instigation of a priest, and other butcheries followed all over Spain.

Finally, the survivors were banished from Spain, and those who took refuge in Portugal fared worse, for their children were taken from them and forcibly baptized. We cannot be surprised that many mothers destroyed their own children rather than leave them to be trained by their persecutors And the victims were the fellow countrymen of the Founder of our religion!

The Germans, who are certainly not fanatical Christians, have invented a new excuse for their barbarities. The Jews are to be banned on eugenic grounds. This is perhaps the most ridiculous pretext ever invented. For the Jews, with the possible exception of the Scotch, are the most highly endowed race in the world in practical ability. The Jews have a very fine record in philosophy, imaginative literature, natural science, and, above all, in music. In painting they excel rather as connoisseurs than as artists. But on the whole, they are perhaps the most gifted race in the world.

I am completely puzzled by this atavistic outbreak in Germany. We can be silly enough ourselves at times; but when we want to be medieval we are content to array our clergy in the Court dress of a Byzantine nobleman; we have got beyond the baiting of Jews, the burning of witches and the torture of witnesses.

IV

MY UTOPIA

THERE is a legend, quite without foundation, that I am fond of finding fault with society as it is, without having anything better to suggest in its place. I have my own vision of a happy future, which may be ours if we want it.

I do not think we are moving in that direction at present, but if our scientific experts are right, we have almost unlimited time before us to make every possible and impossible experiment in social hygiene. It is true that twenty thousand years hence London will probably be under the sea, but I will plant my imaginary society at a date only five hundred or one thousand years hence.

The optimum population of Great Britain has been fixed at twenty million. This is far from saturation point; but several other considerations besides the food supply have been thought of, and it has been decided that the people shall not live in crowds. The majority live in villages and small towns; there are no very large cities except London.

No persons are allowed to marry and have children without certificates of bodily and mental fitness. But since inheritable bodily and mental defects have been almost eradicated, and since there is no recklessly breeding submerged class, very little interference with personal liberty is necessary. The tendency is for the population to remain almost stationary, for large families are neither approved nor desired.

Mental and physical tests are a part of school and university training. These, and family histories, are registered, and an A1 husband or wife is as much sought after as wealth and titles are now. Physical perfection is cultivated, and a rational costume enables beauty to be recognized in the body and limbs as well as in the face.

Not much change is required in women's dress, which is now sensible and becoming, but all cosmetics are sternly forbidden. For men, a cap, tunic, and long stockings, as worn in part of the Middle Ages, are cheap, convenient and graceful. Each trade or profession wears a distinctive badge.

War has been entirely abolished, and all tariff walls. The nations are distinct and independent, but their emulation is friendly, like that of the counties at cricket. Most countries are nearly self-supporting, both in raising food and in manufactures. Improved agriculture has enabled Britain to feed its twenty million without depending on export trade. Food, however, is everywhere cheap and abundant, and, for reasons of health, less of it is consumed per head.

Since there are no wars, no army or navy, no national debt, and no mass-bribery by legislation, the functions of the central government are almost nominal, and national taxes are almost *nil*. The Parliament, which meets for a few weeks every year, is a dignified and elderly senate, composed largely of ex-officials and retired business men. It is an honour to belong to it, since politics are no longer corrupt.

Equality of income is not aimed at, but there are no opportunities of making large fortunes, and no motive for desiring them, since no social prestige is attached to the possession of wealth.

Local taxation is necessarily high, but the citizens get the full benefit from it. Every county supports its own university, with technical and art schools, which are very popular. Sculpture, painting and architecture have reached a high standard of excellence because most of the citizens use their abundant leisure in practising arts and crafts, unless they prefer to study literature or science.

Each parish has its own public garden, recreation ground, gymnasium, swimming-pool, school and library. Each parish has also a large hall, which on week-days is used for public meetings, concerts, theatricals, cinema shows, lectures and readings from good literature. On Sundays a screen is rolled back, revealing an apse fitted for (I hope) united public worship.

Crime is very rare, and is never punished by imprisonment. There are reformatories for first offenders, and incorrigibly anti-social persons are privately and painlessly extinguished, without humiliation to their families.

The clergy are all trained in the psychology of religion, and it is recognized that the most important part of their duties is giving individual advice and help to those who are in trouble about their souls, and who wish to overcome their special temptations. In this work of individual guidance I should call the interviews consultations, not confessions. Some of the clergy would win reputations as consulting physicians, and theirs would be a full-time job; but in many villages the parson would also follow some secular calling. He might be the schoolmaster or parish doctor.

Wireless has, in my community, partially superseded lectures and concerts, but not entirely, since the people like to meet in their hall and see the performers. It is not uncommon for a new book to be read aloud on the wireless.

Newspapers are fewer in number than they are to-day, since party politics hardly exist. Great popular interest is roused by new scientific discoveries, by journals devoted to the arts and crafts, and by descriptions of foreign countries. Distant lands may be very easily visited during the week-end, for the airplanes can cover three hundred miles an hour.

A universal language has been established for international intercourse, and is taught in the schools everywhere as a second language. By

248

an immense majority, American (fortunately still intelligible in England) was chosen as the common speech of mankind.

The twentieth century is still looked back upon as the great age of scientific discovery. Television and the abolition of smoke were already achieved in this century. Since then, the most important improvement has been the extirpation of microbic diseases, with the exception of the common cold, which still remains the opprobrium of medical science.

Campaigns against these pests became possible only when the whole world placed itself under the control of the League of Nations, which, relieved from its primary object of preventing war, was henceforth mainly occupied in questions of public health, friendly intercourse between nations, and international trade.

One disease was attacked after another, and some hardship was inevitable while the sufferers were segregated. In a few cases, a disease which was supposed to have been destroyed broke out again from unknown causes; but these sporadic outbreaks were easily dealt with.

Well, that is my dream of a possible future. I am no disbeliever in progress, but I very heartily disbelieve in a law of progress. A religious writer said, "Ye are as holy as ye truly wish to be holy." In the same way, we can be as civilized as we truly wish to be civilized.

V

NO MORE REVOLUTIONS

MR. EVERETT D. MARTIN, an American, has written
a book with the attractive title, *Farewell to Revolution.*

The earlier part of the volume will not satisfy
historians. The faction fights of the ancient Greek
cantons inspired Plato and Aristotle with very
acute reflections on the cycles of political changes.
They saw that the destruction of privilege paves
the way for what they called tyranny. But there
was no similarity between ancient Greece and
modern Europe; Greek life and politics have only
once been revived—in medieval Italy. Still less
can the decline and fall of the Roman Empire
suggest any instructive parallels.

I think, however, that he is right when he
says that the cycle of the long popular struggle for
liberty, equality and fraternity has at last been
closed.

Revolution means the triumph, and the enslavement, of the crowd. It means that liberty is dead—
all that men have struggled for since the ancient
republic of Athens.

All revolutions have been the work of small
desperate minorities. They are not the work of a
class at all, but of a well-organized conspiracy,

which has mastered the technique of propaganda and terrorism.

The "class-conscious proletariat" does not exist.

The French Government in 1793 was a minority government. It was not, as has been often asserted, a bourgeois government. Out of twelve thousand persons executed, seven thousand five hundred were small farmers, artisans and tradesmen.

It seems that many people suppose that the Bolshevist revolution was directed against the Tsar. The Tsar had disappeared long before. The *coup d'état* took place on the eve of the calling of a national convention, authorized to draw up a democratic constitution—a convention to which only a hopelessly small minority of Bolshevists had been elected.

The French Revolution of 1789 caused more alarm in Europe than the outbreak of cholera. It was a new disease, like the hideous malady which appeared in Europe about 1495.

Since then, revolution has been endemic, with occasional epidemic outbreaks.

The psychology of crowd-contagion remains rather mysterious; but this is no reason for being content with explanations which are demonstrably untrue. Historians are poor hands at predicting the future, but they have a power, not claimed even by the Deity, of altering the past. They always back the winner—after the race.

The legend of the misery of the French peasantry

in the eighteenth century is too deeply rooted to be easily disturbed. But, in fact, France was the richest country in Europe, and, in spite of the extravagance of the court and the scandalous wealth of the higher clergy, prosperity was widely distributed.

Rousseau, poisonous sentimentalist as he was, says nothing about the state of the peasantry.

Arthur Young is not nearly so severe as those who have not read him suppose.

In 1880 was published a book of letters from Dr. Rigby, a practical farmer, who travelled in France in the summer of 1789. Between Calais and Lille "every acre was in a state of the highest cultivation." "The wheat crops are superior to any which can be produced in England." "The people are strong and well made, and they all look happy." "We have seen few signs of opulence; but we have seen few of the lower classes in rags, idleness and misery."

When he went on to Germany he found all the evils which he had been led to think existed in France. "How every country and every people we have seen since we left France sink in comparison with that animated country."

The reign of Louis XVI had been a period of bold remedial legislation; in two generations the cultivators had bought and owned one-third of the soil.

It is hardly ever desperation which causes revolutions; they occur on a rising market, when for some reason or other the government is weak.

Three tendencies, says Lothrop Stoddard, bring down civilization—structural overloading, when the apparatus becomes too costly and elaborate; biological regression, when, as usually happens, the survival rate is thoroughly dysgenic; and the revolt of the underworld. Civilization always throws up large numbers of the uncivilizable. Some are a reversion to savagery; others are degenerate— imbecile, neurotic or epileptic. Others are border-liners, who just cannot make good. These all hate the civilization in which they can find no place. Normally they are kept down by law and custom, but as soon as the bonds of society begin to dissolve they seize their chance.

They find capable leaders, not of their own sort. The leaders of social revolutions are never working men. They are often criminals. They are generally middle-class intellectuals, and almost always very young.

The psychology of the *enragé* is an interesting study. It is the subject of Anatole France's brilliant novel, *Les Dieux ont soif*.

The typical example is Marx. A consuming hatred of civilized society was the foundation of his character. His political and economic theories were always unsound, and are quite out of date. But he may claim a kind of greatness on two grounds. He realized the power of hatred when it

253

is artificially stimulated and fostered by mass-suggestion; and he laid down with masterly skill the whole technique of revolution.

This technique was carefully studied by the Bolshevists, and carried out in its entirety.

The transformation of childlike glee at the beginning of a revolution into furious hatred and cruelty is very remarkable. As Anatole France says, if you begin by preaching universal fraternity you will end by wanting to kill all who do not agree with you.

The massacres in Russia have far surpassed all previous records. Bela Kun ordered the execution of sixty thousand to seventy thousand people in the Crimea. Soviet records give about one million eight hundred thousand (including eight hundred and fifteen thousand peasants) as the number put to death in the first five years of the revolution.

And then we see English politicians writing books about "a new civilization," and speaking with smug satisfaction, from their comfortable armchairs, of the "liquidation" of the Kulaks. One would almost like to give them a dose of their own medicine.

VI

THE SHADOW OF TO-MORROW

At last I have found a diagnosis of the sickness of civilization which entirely satisfies me. Professor Huizinga of Holland is well known as a philosophical historian, and in this new book, translated by his son (Heinemann, 7s. 6d.), he faces all our dangers gravely, but without despair.

He is not a pessimist.

The scientific concept of evolution, which is now the framework of all our thinking, ought to have taught us that fundamental changes in social life cannot come about suddenly—history affords no examples of such changes, and also that the clock cannot be put back—a return to a glorious past, if a glorious past ever existed, is impossible.

Nevertheless, the present strain upon the social order is greater than at earlier periods of crisis, such as the Reformation and the French Revolution, because there has never before been such a systematic undermining of civilization by a creed of class-warfare. Defeatism is in the air, because the flame of faith and hope burns low.

The part of this book to which I wish to draw special attention is his treatment of the modern State-worship.

The figment of *race*—the superiority of the Nordic

255

or some other pure stock—is a mixture of bad science and stale romanticism. There are no pure races. But this stale romanticism has taken a pestilent form in the idea of the "hero," which in spite of Carlyle has never caught on in this country.

"Here lies a man who tried to do his duty," is the epitaph of a great Englishman. He has no wish to be called a hero, any more than a good man wishes to be called a saint.

But in Germany, and not only in Germany, Nietzsche's picture of the "great blond beast" trampling on his neighbours is very attractive as a national ideal. It implies of course that considerations of right and wrong, of justice and mercy, do not apply to foreign politics. The State can do no wrong.

We can find something like this doctrine in Machiavelli and Hobbes. But until our time the principle was not denied that States owed a sacred duty to obey religion and the divinely sanctioned "law of nature."

There was an international order, based on the old political philosophy, on Christian ethics, the code of chivalry, and juridical theory. The nations, as members of a community, were bound to observe the same rules of conduct as individuals.

They never did so, but it was reserved for our generation to declare that they ought not to do so. We now read, in well-known writers, that "for the external relations of States Christian and social ethics do not apply."

"Any means, however immoral, can legitimately be resorted to for the seizure and preservation of sovereign authority." These two quotations ought to be enough; they are quite typical of the teaching which is encouraged on the Continent.

First, this doctrine has had the natural result of reviving devilish cruelties which had long ago been repudiated by all civilized countries.

It is sometimes said that nations at war will stick at nothing. It is not true. Why did the famous English archers never poison their arrows? Why were wells never poisoned? Why were captive civilians not driven before an attacking force as a shield?

And now! I think most of us will agree with Huizinga when he says, "the fact that bacterial warfare has been seriously considered will remain an everlasting and terrible stigma upon an unworthy generation. If men are to fight each other with such weapons, it will be such a Satanic blasphemy that it will be better for a culpable humanity to perish in its own iniquity." The same may be said of yperite deliberately poured down upon non combatants, women and children.

Second, those who declare that the State can do no wrong seem to think only of their own State. If their enemies behave in the same way, they invoke God and justice and humanity—everything that they have themselves repudiated. The inevitable result must be international anarchy and wars of extermination.

Third, there is not the slightest reason why the State should be the only corporation raised above the laws of right and wrong. We all belong to many societies, some wider, some narrower than the State, each with indefeasible claims upon us. The God-State is a mere idol, a fetish. There can be no doubt whatever that other associations, corporations, parties and factions will claim the same superiority to moral considerations which this atrocious theory demands for the State. It must breed not only wars of extermination between nations, but civil wars and rebellions, marked by all the horrors which we are witnessing in Spain.

Huizinga is right in pointing to this as the evil which may wreck civilization for good and all. He lays his finger on the root of the mischief, and he points to the only remedy. "The new discipline will have to be a surrender to all that can be conceived as the highest. There can be no more nation or class than the individual existence of self. Happy those for whom that principle can only bear the name of Him who said, 'I am the way, the truth and the life'."

HISTORICAL

I

GREEKS AND BARBARIANS

LET us suppose a visitor from another planet sent to make an intelligent study of our Western civilization. What would strike him most? Here, he would say, is a group of peoples, racially closely allied and sharing the same culture. In all the externals of civilization they far surpass anything that has been seen before on their planet. They are in a period of technical perfection in machinery and manufacturing skill, which, as their prophet Goethe said more than a hundred years ago, is the death of art. I see that they try to make beautiful things, but they have lost the knack. It is an ugly civilization.

But this, he would say, is not the most remarkable thing that I found; I realize that mechanicism and consumptionism are destructive of beauty. But when I entered their places of worship, I found the congregations solemnly repeating extracts from the ferociously patriotic literature of an ancient Bedouin tribe. I heard them exhorting each other to think upon Rahab and Babylon, to behold the Philistines and Morians, and invoking blessings on any who should dash the Babylonian children against the stones. They sang a great deal about Jerusalem and Jordan and David, but not a word about London and Thames and King Alfred.

Then I went to their public schools and universities, and found that the staple of their education was the poetry, history and philosophy of an Eastern Mediterranean people who flourished more than two thousand years ago, and of an Italian city the ruler of which described himself as *dominus totius orbis*, his actual possessions being about two per cent of the land surface of the globe.

Surely, he would say, here is a civilization which has not yet found its soul. It is content to borrow and imitate from the ancients, who, as they used to say, have more wit and wisdom than we. Are not Thames and Severn, rivers of England, better than all the waters of Israel? Are not Dante, Shakespeare and Goethe as great poets as Homer, Sophocles and Virgil? Has philosophy made no advance since Plato and Aristotle? Are the tricks of Alcibiades and Nicias to get Hyperbolus ostracized any more important than the squabbles on the London County Council?

Well, Greece was very nearly lost to the West for some seven hundred years. The Dark Ages were really dark, in spite of all attempts to whitewash them. Except for Byzantine architecture—Constantinople was for centuries the only civilized city in Europe except Cordova—would the world have lost much if all the period between A.D. 500 and 1100 had been blotted out? Then came the revival,

in which at first Aristotle filtered through into
Western thought by way of the Arabs, and then
what we truly call the Renaissance, when the West
awakened from a long sleep with the classics in
her hands. "Back to Greece" was the watchword
of the Italian scholars, painters, sculptors, poets
and men of science. But the revived paganism of
the Mediterranean lands scandalized the northern
races, with whom both Hellenism and Latinism
were alien cultures. So in the north, in partial
reaction against the Renaissance, came the Reformation, with the cry, "Back to Palestine." The
Hebrews had a real and indispensable contribution
to make to the progress of civilization, though
Matthew Arnold was right in saying that industrial
England in his time "Hebraized" too one-sidedly.
Our debt to Palestine is not my subject; but
I emphasize that modern Europe put itself into
leading-strings to two masters, who concurrently
gave our civilization its character. The north
rejected Latinism, the south remained under its
influence. This is the great difference between
the Germanic peoples and the Mediterraneans.
But the north did not reject Hellenism. Ever since
the Renaissance we have been under these two
influences, Hellenism and Hebraism. We have *not*
produced an independent culture moulded by the
northern genius. We have only superimposed upon
the traditional pattern a few strange products of
our own, of which chivalry, romance and modern

business are the most remarkable. Whether we are at last escaping from the old models, and whether we are wise in trying to do so, is a question which I shall try to answer briefly before the end of the chapter.

Why do we still pay so much homage to the ideas of two tiny nations of remote antiquity? Because they alone were truly creative. Their best was not borrowed. As Israel rejected Canaanite religion, and at last even Greek religion, so Greece, in the words of Gilbert Murray, "starts clean from nature, with almost no entanglements of creeds, customs and traditions." We need not deny the debt of Greece to Egypt and Crete; the statement remains broadly true. The message of Greece and the message of Palestine are two permanent enrichments of the human race; and we are very far from having exhausted either of these fountain-heads of wisdom.

But what do we mean by Hellenism? Isocrates said that it is the name of a culture, not of a race. This must be our starting-point; otherwise we shall be entangled inextricably in ethnological problems. The Greeks were a race of splendid mongrels. The so-called Pelasgians were, I suppose, a Mediterranean race, akin to the Cretan Minoans, and speaking a language akin to the hitherto unintelligible old Cretan. And the Achaeans were, I suppose, northern invaders, of predominantly Nordic blood. I cannot agree with Dr. Myres that

the Achaeans were Aegeans. I am glad that I have
not to go into these thorny questions. But most
certainly I do not mean by "the Greeks" all who
have spoken or written in Greek. I would even rather
include among them some natural Greeks who
have expressed themselves in other languages. But
this will hardly be necessary. For the permanent
inspiration of Hellenism comes, not only from a
definite locality, but from a definite period. The
time came, all too soon, when Greece was living
Greece no more. It came when the Greeks lost
their liberty, and with it, as Homer says, half
their manhood. And yet, since the loss of liberty
was mainly political and did not extinguish free
thought, Hellenism, though truncated, lived on, in
a fine though imperfect form, through Hellenistic
times. Hellenism can survive tyranny if this does
not destroy freedom of thought and speech. The
death of freedom of speech did not occur till (we
may choose a definite date for convenience) the
closing of the Athenian schools by Justinian. A
regime of oppressive dictatorships, such as we are
now threatened with, would indeed be the death or
eclipse of Hellenism, and a return to "barbarism."
In the same way the Jews gave their treasure to
humanity long ago; the modern Jews are no longer
our prophets—which is no excuse for maltreating
them, for they are still one of the most gifted races
in the world.

Even if we confine our attention to the great

period of Greece, we are obliged to select some features as more characteristic than others. It would be easy to find examples of all the most unhellenic things in Greece—sombre superstitions; even human sacrifice lurking in a few remote places; merely foolish superstitions sometimes spoiling military operations; prosecutions for impiety, even at Athens; callous cruelty on many occasions; Plato's proposal to set up a holy office of the inquisition; sentimental romanticism rampant in Hellenistic times but not unknown before. Nevertheless, these things are not typical; we can find most or all of them in other nations: we find in the Greeks several things of the highest value which we do not find elsewhere.

What did the Greeks themselves value most among the good gifts of the gods? It does not follow that what they wished for they had, or had not. There are some things which are not wished for, because they are taken for granted. We English do not talk much about the best parts of our make-up—our kindliness and toleration; our short memory for injuries; our love of justice and fair play; our hatred of cruelty. We pride ourselves on our business capacity, which is very moderate; our energy and industry, in which we are rather deficient; our political wisdom, which shows itself chiefly in our distrust of logic and our conviction (by no means always right) that "force is no remedy." Similarly the Greeks did not realize

how unique they were in allowing the freedom of
speech of which I have spoken. And yet, where
do we find it except where Greek influence is
manifest? For some eight hundred years, down to
the closing of the schools of Athens, the human
spirit had been free to inquire into all things
in heaven and earth. Under this freedom, and in
consequence of this freedom, philosophy and science
were born and flourished. Since the Renaissance,
mankind has been emancipated again—in a few
favoured countries. At the end of Greek free
thought, a philosopher lamented that "a shapeless
darkness" was extinguishing all the beauty of the
world. Are we on the verge of another dark age?

It is more surprising that the Greeks undervalued
their supreme achievements in art. Aeschylus, when
he wrote his own epitaph, said nothing about
his poetry: he records only that he "did his bit"
at Marathon. Thucydides, in the famous speech
of Pericles, thinks mainly of the glories won by
Athens in the storms in a tea-cup which they called
their wars. When the Athenians came back to
their city after the retreat of the Persians, they
had no scruple about "scrapping" all their old works
of art. They knew they could do better; so did the
Renaissance Italians when they painted over some
glorious pictures. As far as I know, we must wait
for the Hellenistic age, when such masterpieces
were no longer produced, to find really appreciative
literary criticism of the great works of art. And yet

267

criticism was keen and searching. In landscape, said one of them, we are content with general truth of outline, but in the human body every slight failure of the artist to reproduce the perfect contour is at once noticed and criticized. The Greeks knew all about the beauty of the human body; they saw it every day. Under the medieval Church, when men and women were taught to be ashamed of their bodies, we find very delicate representations of vegetable forms, while the human figures (in early medieval art) are grotesque, and show no knowledge of anatomy. It is possible that the new cult of sun-bathing and a minimum of clothing may once more open the eyes of artists to the possibilities in that direction. To the Greeks, the horror of exposing the body was characteristic of barbarians.

The four things that the Greeks, in an often-quoted proverbial saying, desired for themselves were, in the following order—Health, Good Looks, Wealth honestly come by, To be Young with one's Friends. I wonder what most of us would choose. Questionnaires have been held; but who is honest on these occasions? I think I should choose:

1. Wisdom, i.e. knowledge of the relative values of things.
2. Domestic happiness.
3. Recognition and encouragement.

And I am not sure what my fourth would be—

perhaps the welfare of my country. Health might come in a few modern lists; good looks only in those compiled by the fair sex; money we all desire, but are ashamed to avow it; "to be young with one's friends"—yes, for the few years when it is possible. Perhaps it is not fair to take this merry quatrain too seriously, but it commended itself to Greek sentiment.

As for health and good looks, if the Greeks desired them they certainly had them. There is no doubt about their extraordinary beauty. Their statues were somewhat idealized; anatomists have noticed one or two graceful lines which are, now at least, not very common in the human body. But look at the portrait reliefs on their tombs, and their vase paintings. They were a very beautiful race. Another point will interest all students of vital statistics. Take the recorded ages at death of fifty distinguished Greeks in the fifth and fourth centuries. They are far and away higher than the average duration of life until our own generation. The Greeks were extremely hardy and frugal—in Greece itself. In the large and wealthy towns in the Greek colonies there was more indulgence. Plato was disgusted to find that the Syracusans ate two (not three) heavy meals every day. Even the older men took their gymnastic exercises, and kept their figures. Sixty, not fifty, was the age of exemption from military service. The flabby bodies of the barbarians were noticed with displeasure. This bodily perfection was perhaps helped by their habit of exposing the body to the air. The most perfectly formed men I have ever seen were two Zulus in Barnum's show, who danced on the stage almost naked. Except for their negroid features, they were perfect bronze Greek statues. Sir Francis Galton told me that the English athletes whom he had seen unclothed were all imperfectly formed about the legs, and I have noticed the same in cricket changing rooms at Cambridge. Even the statues of Michael Angelo and his contemporaries seem to me inferior to the Greek statues in the development of the lower limbs.

In literature their pre-eminence has been generally acknowledged. "In every branch of letters and learning," says Cicero, "they are our masters." "Their work," says Goethe, "is marked by grandeur, excellence, sanity, humanity, a high philosophy of life, a powerful intuition." Livingstone quotes Wordsworth as saying, "Beside Aeschylus and Sophocles I am nothing"; and Shelley, "The period between the birth of Pericles and the death of Aristotle is undoubtedly, whether considered in itself or in the effects which it has produced on the destinies of civilized men, the most memorable in the history of the world." Mill says that "the Greeks were the beginners of nearly everything, Christianity excepted, of which the modern world makes its boast." Macaulay's unabated enthusiasm for the Greek classics is known to readers of his life.

Livingstone finds the essential qualities of Greek literature to be Simplicity, Perfection of Form, Truth and Beauty. The Greeks were simple, partly because they were not sophisticated by long traditions and refinements of culture, and partly because for mechanical reasons their books had to be comparatively short. (The Fathers of the Church and the schoolmen, however, lived long before printing, and were certainly not short!) This simplicity is generally delightful, but occasionally it jars badly. Odysseus has not a word of farewell for Nausicaa, who reveals in the most charming way that she is half in love with him; he wastes no tenderness on Circe or Calypso; Antigone in Sophocles argues that it is better to lose a husband than a brother, because she might marry again, but "as my parents are in Hades, I cannot have another brother"; and Socrates replies to the tearful lament of his wife on the day of his execution, "Let someone take her away." When all is said and done, the Greeks were more than a little hard. "The great Greek dramas," says Mrs. O. W. Campbell, "lack tenderness, and except in a very limited direction they lack passion. They could teach courage and conscience; they could not teach hope and love."

Their psychology is rather naïve. They seldom realized the beauty of strangeness and irregularity. I have sometimes been afraid that they would have admired a monkey-puzzle more than a beech.

They certainly liked clear-cut consistency in character. They would have admired *King Lear*, but I think Hamlet's vacillation would have made them impatient.

Their technique is usually very fine, though the prose of Thucydides is harsh and clumsy, and the choruses of Aeschylus are as difficult as *Sordello*. The creation of the Homeric hexameter and of the Iambic trimeter are marvellous achievements.

Greek truthfulness to nature was not brutal realism. There were conventions, and there was deliberate selection. They wrote objectively, and were very sparing of comments. Think of Thucydides' colourless narrative of the failure at Amphipolis, which ruined him professionally. Who would think that the Thucydides who came a day too late was the historian himself? They did not describe disgusting things, like Zola and his followers. To make a plot or a character unpleasant was an artistic defect; to *say everything* in poetry was bad taste. The restraint in their best epitaphs is marvellous. I need hardly say that the man with the muck-rake is entirely unrepresented in Greek literature before the decadence. The Rabelaisian jokes of Aristophanes were just part of the fun of the fair. Greek literature, as a whole, is very clean. Think by contrast of Petronius, Boccaccio, Rabelais, and even Anatole France.

Livingstone finds it a merit in the Greeks that they do not *preach*, like our English writers, many of whom—such as Thomas Huxley, Wells, and Shaw—are parsons *manqués*. There is, however, another side to this. Part of the "Hebraism" (as Matthew Arnold calls it) of our civilization is that most of us are interested in what we call "causes." We want to change things and make them better. We have our own nostrums—a revival of religion, better education, humanitarianism, socialism and what not. Whatever our pet remedy may be, we wish to advocate it. Most of our writers would find their occupation gone without this motive; not Scott or Shakespeare, perhaps, but certainly Wordsworth, Carlyle, Ruskin and Dickens, besides those already mentioned. Now broadly speaking the Greeks had no "causes." They took the world as it was, and tried either to enjoy and make the best of it, or (almost all of them after Aristotle) to make themselves invulnerable in one way or another. It seems to me a signal superiority of Christianity that it does not try to make us invulnerable. We allow the evils of life to hurt us, to hurt us badly, and that makes us desire to cure them. You see, I am not holding up Hellenism as a complete guide to life. I shall have a little more to say about this presently. But let me quote one passage from Thucydides (Bk. 3) to illustrate the acquiescence of the wisest Greeks in evils which we hope to be remediable: "The class-war at Corcyra grew more savage, and made a peculiar impression

because it was the first outbreak of an upheaval
which spread through almost the whole of Greek
society. . . . It brought one calamity after another
upon the States of Greece, calamities which occur,
and will continue to occur, as long as human
nature remains the same, however they may be
modified or occasionally mitigated by changes
of circumstance." If this is true, "let us flee hence
to our dear country," wherever our heaven may
be. Thucydides in this book brings a terrible indictment against his countrymen. But a long war,
especially a civil war, will make any nation cruel
and treacherous. The Romans would have destroyed
Athens after Aegospotami; even the Spartans refused
to do this.

The flowering times of humanity have been
the brief periods when mankind finds itself at home
in its world. They never last long. The tree of
knowledge drives us out of every paradise in turn.
"These obstinate questionings of outward things"
forbid us to rest content. All progress, it has been
said, is due to the fact that men are never content
to live within their income. In the formative
period the Greek mind was confident and at peace
with itself, dreading excess above everything else,
and with very little sense of sin.

The city State seems to be very favourable for
the development of genius, as we see when the
same conditions were reproduced in medieval Italy;
but it is terribly wasteful of its human material.

From the historical point of view, the fatal draw-
back in Greek civilization was that it was *unicellular*.
There was no tendency to form large units; and
when the Greeks spread themselves over Asia
in the populous towns of the Hellenistic kings,
though the race was still partly Hellenic, the culture
was so no longer. Why did they never think of
representative government? Plato's last ideal was
something like the late lamented British constitution;
but he nowhere suggests representation.

Still we must not blame the Greeks for not solving
a problem which is far as ever from being solved
to-day. Plato, like Ruskin, was a true-blue Tory
socialist; he would burn no incense to democracy;
he had seen the fetish at too close quarters. He, was,
up to a point, pro-Spartan, as many Englishmen
admired the German system before the war. He
wanted a strong government, an articulated hierarchy; and the judge of wisdom and folly was to
be the one best man in the State. Aristotle appealed
instead to the man of sense, to educated public
opinion. I suppose this is the better side of the Fascist
ideal, which is to make an end, once for all, of
class-warfare, and to rationalize government. Plato's
grand Idea was to give the power to a class who
were to have neither the will nor the opportunity
to misuse it for their own aggrandizement. He
was just as much a typical Greek as his disciple
Ruskin was a typical Englishman. He does not
represent at all the turn which things were actually

275

taking. The nearest approach to Plato's republic so far is the medieval Latin theocracy, which until the Renaissance owed very little to Greece.

I have called my paper "Greeks and Barbarians." We, of course, are the barbarians. The word meant "foreigners," whose unintelligible speech sounded like "Bar, bar." Ovid in exile uses the word in this sense. "Barbarus hic ego sum, quia non intelligor ulli." It seems to have been the Athenians of the fifth century who began to use the word contemptuously. Herodotus in his earlier books generally calls the Persians "the Persians"; in his later books, after he had been at Athens, they are generally "the barbarians." At first the Romans accepted the word of themselves. But Rome was never quite outside the Hellenic pale; the Senate could consult the Delphic oracle. Matthew Arnold called the English upper class "barbarians," though they are really the best Greeks in Europe. They are handsome, and train their bodies; they are devoted to athletics, and they know no language except their own.

Well, what have we barbarians still to learn from the Greeks? We have, as I have said, other teachers, from Palestine. We are often told that Judaism was a religion of hope. St. Paul says truly that the Jews "against hope believed in hope." They were free from that deep scepticism about Providence which beset the Greeks. They did not worship Fortune. They would not have

276

approved of the Greek epigram which Lord
Brougham translated for his villa at Cannes:
"I've entered port; fortune and hope adieu;
make game of others, for I've done with you,"
nor with "There's nothing new or true, and no
matter." No; "the most High ruleth among the
kingdoms of men." Still, when writers like Mr.
Edwyn Bevan father on the Jewish tradition the
modern belief in progress, they forget how entirely
that belief was wanting in the Christian Church
till modern times. For the Jew, the arm of the
Lord was revealed catastrophically. I am inclined
to think that the belief in the regeneration of
society by concerted human effort is our distinctively
modern contribution to practical philosophy.

To Christianity, before it was Europeanized
and Hellenized, we owe the teaching which puts
love or sympathy in the place of honour among the
virtues instead of justice—a change of immense
importance. We owe to it also the lesson of gain
through pain, of victory through defeat, the
"offence of the Cross." Suffering is to be met,
welcomed and overcome. I will not speak of other
Christian doctrines, because long before the end
of the first century the two rivers of Greek and
Hebrew thought had begun to flow together.
Christianity, as Clement of Alexandria said, is a
river which has received affluents from all sides.
Nor, from our present point of view, can we
regard later Greek thought as purely Hellenic.

Alexandria was a melting-pot of religions and philosophies.

Well, apart from these traditions, what are the ideals and ideas of our own time? Humanism, you will say, and chiefly scientific humanism. Some, chiefly in the name of science, object to humanism; a larger number say, Humanism by all means, but why Greek humanism? The Greeks mixed up art, gymnastics and dancing with religion. They would have opened the Wimbledon tournament with a sacrifice, and accompanied the games on the flute. If the King's horse happened to win the Derby, he would have ordered Mr. John Masefield to write a hymn about it. Their greatest statues were of the gods. That is not our way of looking at art and athletics. Your cult of the classics (they say) is old-fashioned. We remember Dean Gaisford's Christmas sermon at Christ Church. "Nor can I do better in conclusion than impress upon you the study of Greek literature, which not only elevates above the vulgar herd, but leads not infrequently to positions of considerable emolument." We rather agree (they will say) with the Principal of the University of Louvain in *The Vicar of Wakefield*. "You see, young man, that I never learned Greek, and I don't find that I ever missed it. I have had a doctor's cap and I have ten thousand florins a year without Greek; I eat heartily without Greek. In short, as I do not know Greek, I don't believe there is any good

in it." Cobden said he would give the whole of
Thucydides for one copy of *The Times*. (I believe,
if we include the advertisements, the number of
words is about the same.) Frederick William
of Prussia once burst into the room where his
son was reading the classics with his tutor, and
laid about him with a cane.

Well, humanism is not enough. It gives us no
standard except hedonism and humanitarianism,
and these do not necessarily belong to it. We need
a background of the eternal and absolute values,
which sceptical relativism denies at its peril.
Humanism without Platonism generally ends in
pessimism, and a Platonist who is not a bit of
a Puritan is a dilettante. The fatal question,
"Well, why shouldn't I?" gets no satisfactory
answer.

We have still a great deal to learn from the Greeks.
I will go into particulars. Our life is far too compli-
cated. We increase our wants and demands upon
society quite irrationally. We like to have everything
done for us. We shall soon have a population who
cannot walk or read or write or think. A drastic
simplification of life would improve our health,
our minds and our characters.

Under the influence of industrialism, we have
taken as our motto "everything too much." The
Greeks did not believe that there is something
fine in every superlative. They did not believe that
a nation which travels sixty miles an hour is

necessarily six times as civilized as one which travels only ten.

Democracy speaks with contempt of intellectuals and high-brows, and has brought the daily papers with the largest circulation to the lowest depth of fatuity and vulgarity. Rabindranath Tagore, after a visit to the United States, thus records his experiences. Democracy "makes a deliberate study of the dark patches of the human intellect, wherewith to help itself to create an atmosphere of delusion through hints, gestures, yells and startling grimaces, for the purpose of stupefying the popular mind. When I was in Chicago, I saw everywhere on the town walls one single name blazoned in big letters in an endless round of repetition, like the whirlwind monotony of a dervish dance that dazes one's mind into vacuity. Evidently the name belonged to some candidate for popular election. But what an insult to the people, who are supposed to represent the supreme power in their government, openly to apply to them the spell of hypnotism in place of reason, as the medicine-man does in the heart of Africa!"

Lo, the poor Indian! They didn't know everything down in Judee, nor at Benares, nor at Athens. The masses at Athens went to hear Sophocles and Euripides, and recitations of Homer. They believed with Longinus that great writing is the echo of a great soul, and with Yeats that style is high breeding in words and arguments.

And if the repudiation of Greek ideals has produced ugly results in social life—in eating and clothing and avoidance of bodily and mental exertion; if it has degraded our politics and vulgarized our popular literature; what are we to say of the anti-Greek movement in art? Would that Ruskin were alive to deal faithfully with the drivellers who bid us seek our models in the "art" of the savages of Benin, or the statues of Easter Island; who bid us adorn the façades of public buildings with female figures apparently suffering from elephantiasis, and sometimes give us a canvas scrawled with geometrical zig-zags. The whole thing is manifestly a disease. Some of the new architecture is not much better. A child could produce a model, with a box of bricks, just like a modern pile of flats. As Sir Reginald Blomfield has said, "In the arts" (and he might include the greatest art, the art of living) "there are no short cuts, and anarchy, the destruction of what has been won for us in the past, is not advance but the straight road to the bottomless pit of barbarism."

But above all let us remember that there has been a time when we English could make our own the boast of Pericles: "Our city as a whole is an education for Greece, and our citizens, man for man, have no equals for freedom of spirit, versatility of achievement and entire self-sufficiency of body and mind." That freedom, over the greater part of the civilized world, has been wholly lost. The new dictatorships are far more tyrannical, more searching in their inquisitional terrorism, than the rule of any tsar, sultan or emperor. A completely mechanical society would be a servile State in which all spiritual and intellectual life would be strangled. The consummation of this type of polity may be studied in the beehive or the termites' nest.

II

GREAT MEN

"THE world knows nothing of its greatest men." That may be true, but how can we tell? If we know nothing about them, we cannot tell whether they were great. But there is a good chance that, by the time the world knows about them, they have ceased to be great.

A man usually does his best work just before he is found out. If he has done anything very well, there is a conspiracy to prevent him from doing it again. He becomes a celebrity, and the lion-hunters give him no peace. It must be owned that sometimes he likes it.

There are two opposite tendencies—hero-worship, and a desire to pull heroes off their pedestals. The former appeals to romantics, the latter to realists.

Whenever a great movement occurs, whether in the world of ideas or of politics, men choose their representative, and attribute everything to him. If he is a prophet, his disciples make him a peg on which to hang their own best thoughts, or those which they think the best, so that it becomes almost impossible to be sure what he really said or thought.

On a small scale an entirely fictitious character, like George A. Birmingham's General John Regan, may become a legendary hero.

In politics, especially in revolutions, there is great luck in being under the tree when the apple is ready to fall. Lenin's published utterances do not give the impression of much ability, but he is almost a god in Russia. He was a ruthless fanatic, at a moment when ruthless fanaticism was the winning card.

How far were Buddha and Mohammed created by their followers? How far was Socrates created by Plato and Samuel Johnson by Boswell? The two last would have been almost forgotten but for the genius of their loyal admirers.

Carlyle, a great romanticist, thought that history is made by a few great men. Colonel John Buchan gives us a very different picture of one of Carlyle's heroes, Oliver Cromwell—a not very clear-headed opportunist, a rather typical English gentleman, not first-rate in any way except as a cavalry leader. His portrait of the Protector is convincing; Carlyle's is not.

So there has been a violent reaction against the romanticist view of history. Lytton Strachey, who had an animus against the Victorians, writes with a vicious determination to belittle them all. He is amusingly unfair to Arnold of Rugby, unpardonably unfair to General Gordon. He evidently wished to guy Queen Victoria, but could not keep it up.

Wells seems to hate all great men, especially if they wear crowns or epaulettes. He will hardly admit that Julius Caesar and Napoleon were really great.

Here I cannot agree. These men had their opportunities, of course, for which they had to thank their luck or their star; but they were intellectual and practical giants. So, I have no doubt, was Marlborough, that curiously unpopular hero to whom George Trevelyan and Winston Churchill have done tardy justice.

Obviously estimates of comparative greatness vary enormously. Some admire men of thought, others men of action; they can hardly be weighed in the same scales. For instance, the year 1809 will be for ever memorable for having given birth to three of the greatest Englishmen of the last century —Gladstone, Tennyson and Darwin. Which of the three do we rank highest? The fame of Darwin has worn best, though I have no patience with the curs of criticism who yelp at the heels of Tennyson; and as for Gladstone, I was brought up to think him a wicked Radical, but what would we not give to have him back now? Our consciences and our purses would be safe in his keeping. But the great naturalist is the most secure of immortality, Mendel has no more shaken his fame than Einstein has injured Newton.

One or two more remarks may be made about greatness. Some of the giants seem to have had old heads on young shoulders, and to have aged prematurely. Napoleon, no doubt, suffered from cancer long before his death, but he seems to have been nearly played out before Waterloo. His generals were dismayed at his indecision during the Moscow campaign of 1812; and he was only fifty-two when he died in 1821.

Alexander the Great was another precocious genius. If he had lived even as long as Napoleon he would probably have altered the whole course of history. For instance, he would very likely have destroyed Rome. That microbe at Babylon little knew what it was doing. There was no sign of failing power in Julius Caesar, who was about fifty-six when he was murdered.

The case of Shakespeare is remarkable. Why did he stop writing plays after producing *The Tempest*? He was only forty-seven, and he had five more years to live. Why has nobody suggested that he was writing the works of Francis Bacon?

Another reflection is that posterity cannot judge of the overwhelming personal impression that many great men have exercised. A good example is the elder William Pitt, Earl of Chatham. His portraits show his hawk-like features, his large nose, his glowing eyes; but we rely on contemporary records for what we know of his ascendancy over the House of Commons. On one occasion a member rose to assault him as he left the House. Pitt looked at him and he sat down.

Goethe must have possessed this power to a remarkable degree. When Napoleon met him, he exclaimed, "Voilà un homme!" and he never forgot him.

But after all, history is not much more than *une fable convenue.* There would be some very strange surprises if the recording angel were to publish his documents. It is therefore vain to think much of the verdict of posterity, though there is something fine in Francis Bacon's will, in which he commits his name and memory "to men's charitable speeches, to foreign nations, and the next ages"; and still more in Kepler's words, "I can well wait a century for a reader, since God has waited six thousand years for a discoverer."

The finest spirits have felt, "with me it is a very small thing that I should be judged of you or of man's day." Those "of whom the world was not worthy" have generally received far more kicks than halfpence. "Qu'est-ce que la gloire?" says Flaubert. "Faire dire beaucoup de bêtises sur son compte."

III

DOES HUMAN NATURE CHANGE?

RECENT events have shown that humanity is only
skin-deep. For instance, in the winter of 1934 six
million Russian peasants were allowed to die of
hunger in a world glutted with food; their government was selling wheat abroad. We used to think
that Jew-baiting was a medieval pastime; now we
know better.

There is not the slightest reason why human
nature should change, unless the environment
favours the survival of some types and the disappearance of others. Ruling races generally rule
themselves out; nothing fails like success. So a
nation may become milder and less combative;
sheep on the whole have a greater survival value
than wolves. But there is not much use in the sheep
passing resolutions in favour of vegetarianism while
there are still wolves who like mutton. Science in
all its branches advances steadily. In these matters
each generation stands on the shoulders of the last;
progress is cumulative. But there need be no intrinsic progress, no improvement of the human
material, at all. Changes in our bodies are going
on, but very slowly. Our jaws are getting smaller,
our teeth worse; we are beginning to shed our
toe-nails. Our social adaptation to modern civiliza-

tion may be equally slow—almost imperceptible, in fact. It may even be in the wrong direction; for while we employ all our ingenuity in altering our environment, we take no trouble at all to improve the breed of men, and interfere only to prevent natural selection from weeding our garden. If we liked, we might have an army of human mastiffs for policemen, of human greyhounds for postmen, and so on.

"In history," says Professor Freeman, "every step in advance has been also a step backwards." We might try this feat on an escalator, while we are digesting that noble moral maxim, "Stand on the right, and let others pass you." But the favourite theory in antiquity was that the pulse of the universe beats in alternate expansions and contractions. There are great cycles of advance and decline; in the universe as a whole there can be neither progress nor decay.

This theory commends itself to me: I used to think that the stars, after passing through the heat of youth and the cooling blood of old age, might after a long rest be jolted by collisions into renewed vigour, so that the universe may go on for ever. Jeans and Eddington will not let me believe this, they say the world is running down like a clock, and nothing can wind it up again. But I refuse to be convinced; somebody or something wound it up once, and why not again?

Until the eighteenth century, almost everybody

was content to believe that "the thing that hath been is the thing that shall be." Seneca says: "Our ancestors complained of the degeneracy of the age, just as we do. Our posterity will do the same. In reality things do not move at all."

The Emperor Marcus Aurelius thought that a man of forty, if he is moderately intelligent, may be said to have seen all that is past and all that is to come. Hume says: "The world is probably mortal, passing from infancy to old age, and man will share in its changes; but these are too slow to be discerned in the short period known to history. Mankind is no doubt changing slowly, but whether he is advancing or declining we cannot tell."

Goethe "sees the time coming when God will take no more pleasure in the race, and will again proceed to a rejuvenated creation. But we may still for thousands of years enjoy ourselves on our dear old playground, such as it is."

These great men spoke the language of sober good sense. But in the second half of the eighteenth century a delirious apocalyptic dream seized upon Western Europe.

"The flower of humanity," wrote the philosopher Herder, "captive still in its germ, will blossom out one day into the true form of man." The astronomer Herschel declared that "man's progress towards a higher state need never fear a check, but must continue to the very end of history." Herbert Spencer exclaims: "Always towards perfection is the mighty movement towards a complete development and a more unmixed good." Even Darwin hardly realized that his theory of evolution had nothing to do with moral values. It only taught that the true idea is the idea that prevails, and this leaves us with no criterion at all.

When we have cleared our minds of these superstitions about a coming millennium on earth, and consider the changes in the mentality of the Western nations which have become apparent in our day, without asking whether they are intrinsic or (as is much more probable) merely environmental, we shall find, I think, that men act more in masses than they used to do. Everything and everybody is standardized; the herd cramps and stunts the individual. The middle-class ideal of the last century, that the good citizen works hard, lives simply and saves one-third of his income, is discredited not only in practice but in theory.

The higher kind of religion was injured by the war; but every kind of silly superstition flourishes like a green bay-tree. The young people do not seem to care about money, what they do care about it is not easy to say, but they want to look all facts in the face and form their own conclusions. Ostentation has gone quite out of fashion; if democracy is a form of society, not of government, we are becoming more democratic. Some of these changes are for the better, others possibly for the worse. They are not changes in human nature, but reactions to an altered environment.

We must be content to take human nature as it is, without expecting to see any perceptible change in it. For the Christian, human nature has infinite possibilities. But religion has not much visible effect on society as a whole, because the narrow gate has to be passed, and "few there be that find it."

EDUCATION

I

OXFORD

Is there really an Oxford manner? If there is, how does it differ from a Cambridge manner? The students of the two universities come from the same homes and the same schools. Three years seems a short time in which to pick up manners and mannerisms which will stamp them for life.

An unsympathetic critic noted a distinction between the two seats of learning. The Oxford man, he said, looks as if the world belonged to him; the Cambridge man looks as if he did not care to whom it belonged. I think this impression comes from America.

But there is no doubt that there is something in the Oxford manner which has attracted attention, and that it is no new thing. Cardinal Newman, nearly a hundred years ago, said plaintively: "I cannot myself make out how an Oxford man should be known from another. It is a fearful thing that we, as it were, exhale ourselves with every breath we draw."

J. R. Green unkindly says of the Oxonian: "He is not as other men are. He has a deep, quiet contempt for other men. Oxford is his home, and beyond Oxford lie only waste regions of shallowness and inaccuracy."

"They entered the world," says Dr. Johnson, "prepared to show wisdom by their discourse and moderation by their silence, to instruct the modest with easy gentleness, and repress the ostentatious by seasonable superciliousness."

I think myself that these characteristics are occasionally found at Thebes as well as at Athens. Oxford men are fond of comparing their rival to the Boeotian town, the inhabitants of which were supposed to suffer intellectually from the thick atmosphere which they breathed. I cannot say that the climate of Oxford bears much resemblance to the limpid air of Attica; all the more credit to those who have made the English Athens the home of sweetness and light. But for some reason Oxford has always been more in the public eye than Cambridge, and the Oxford manner may be only a salient example of what might as well be called the public-school manner.

The two universities are much more like each other than either of them is like any other place in the world. It is only when one passes from one to the other, as I have done—I was an undergraduate at Cambridge, a college don at Oxford, and then a professor at Cambridge—that one appreciates certain differences between them.

When I returned to Cambridge, Dr. Swete, the Regius Professor of Divinity, was talking to me about the learned Dr. Driver of Oxford. "Did you ever find a mistake in his writings?" he said. That seemed to me a very Cantabrigian compliment. Minute accuracy was more valued at Cambridge; at Oxford philology was subordinate to philosophy with its broad generalizations. Mathematics were a little tyrannical at Cambridge, logic and metaphysics at Oxford.

The Kaiser has not lately had many opportunities of congratulating the Oxford crew on their superior style of rowing. But the prizes in the great professions more often go to Oxford than to Cambridge. This is notably true of the Church. Nearly all the more important bishoprics are held by Oxford men, and I do not think there has been any unfairness. I am inclined to think that good writing, and possibly good speaking, are better taught at Oxford.

It has sometimes been said that Oxford produces "movements," Cambridge only distinguished individuals. The new "group movement," whether one likes it or not, has really no right to use the name of Oxford; its type is transatlantic. But the "Oxford Movement" which began about one hundred years ago could not have been started at Cambridge, which only produced the now forgotten "Simeonites."

On the other hand, Macaulay points out that most of the Reformers came from Cambridge. "Cambridge produced them," he says, "Oxford burnt them." Another Cambridge man, Mr. Birrell, claims quite truly that in poets Cambridge wins in a canter; it is not easy to say why. But neither university treated its singers very kindly. Oxford expelled its star performer, Shelley. Cambridge left Byron to the congenial company of his bear, nearly turned Coleridge into a heavy dragoon, and as for Gray, when the young barbarians of Peterhouse found that the author of the *Elegy* was nervous about fire, and had rigged up a fire-escape from his college window, they raised the alarm one cold winter's night, and the poet slid down his escape into a water-butt which they had placed ready to receive him.

There is, happily, no reason to fear for the future of the old universities. The colleges are full to overflowing, and hundreds of boys from the State schools are assisted every year by grants of public money to finish their education at these places, which are no longer a preserve for the wealthy and professional classes. This, of course, causes a serious congestion in all the professions except the Church, and even in the Church it will soon be difficult for young men to enter the ministry, unless they have good abilities.

We cannot regret this, though it increases the anxieties of the professional parent, who sees one opening after another blocked against his children. The idle, sporting undergraduate will soon be only a memory.

The patrons of the B.B.C. may not like the Oxford speech, but no true Englishman can fail to be proud of Oxford, one of the most beautiful cities in the world. Nor should there be any serious doubt of the value of an Oxford education, for those who wish to profit by it. It is a liberal education, in the old sense of the word; that is to say, it does not train specialists for any trade or profession. Its aim is to improve the mind, and make it a good instrument for whatever work it may be put to.

It is a rash thing for me to express an opinion on these great matters, but I think that since the death of Lotze, Oxford has done more first-rate original work in philosophy than the German universities. The philosophical spirit is not by any means confined to those who are teaching and reading for "Greats." The eminent Professor A. N. Whitehead, himself a Cambridge man, has said, "The University of Oxford has one supreme merit. For centuries she has produced bands of scholars who treated learning imaginatively."

The last word may make us pause. But it means that Oxford recognizes the poetry and spirituality of knowledge. It will never put quantity in the place of quality; it will stand firm against that mechanical standardization of men and things which threatens to ruin what is most precious in European civilization. Europe stands for quality, not quantity; and Oxford is one of the chief citadels of fine thinking and fine living.

CRIMES AGAINST THE KING'S ENGLISH

IT is probable that no language is so carelessly written by men of letters as English. French authors are far more careful. Their ambition is to be elected to the Académie Française, and two or three of the "howlers" which may be and have been collected from our most popular authors would destroy their chances completely.

It happens that very few of our most famous writers have had a university education. Many of them began as journalists, and so formed a habit of writing much too fast. Their style has great merits; it is lucid and vigorous, but seldom beautiful and often incorrect. It is exceptional to find a modern writer who is master of so perfect a prose style as Lowes Dickinson or W. H. Hudson.

Some of the best of living writers are Americans, such as Santayana and Thornton Wilder; and we might name others, like Lippmann, Irving Babbitt, Stoddard and East, who write correctly and very effectively.

Among our best known authors Shaw and Galsworthy are impeccable, Wells not always, though he writes very well when he gives himself time.

A short list of blunders by great authors may be amusing and consoling to some of us.

Carlyle did not know the difference between *euphuism* and *euphemism*. Possibly a few of my readers may share his ignorance. Euphemism means the substitution of a vague or mild expression for a harsh one; euphuism is the name of an affected style, overcharged with antithesis and similes.

Hardy uses *predicate* for *predict*. Dickens is a mine of howlers—e.g. *trustful* for *trustworthy*, *complaisant* for *complacent*, *aggravated* for *irritated*, *mutual* (friend) for *common*; and he can write "nobody will miss her *like* I shall."

Thackeray falls into a common trap when he writes: "Attempting once to scold her in public, Rebecca hit upon the plan of answering her in French." It was Miss Pinkerton, not Rebecca, who attempted the scolding.

This inadvertence in the use of participles sometimes produces very funny results. Huxley writes: "A molecular charge is propagated to the muscles, and causing them to contract the act of retraction is brought about." And what a jingle in the last clause!

But my prize specimen is this. "The most important of the rock-cut tombs are the magnificent examples at Petra. Out in the vertical side of the cliff, and rising sometimes to a hundred feet in height, the artist was freed from the trammels of ordinary construction."

Byron was once guilty of "there let him *lay*," a really colossal solecism. But even the Authorized

Version contains a comparatively venial example of the same blunder—"because she *overlaid* it." And the odious commercialism "same" for "it" derives some sort of sanction from the Prayer Book, e.g. in the Collect for the Conversion of St. Paul.

Editors usually have their own rules about styles; they are severe upon certain solecisms, not the worst, by any means. There was a campaign against "reliable," which is doubtless incorrect; "trustworthy" is a synonym, and much better. But other adjectives which are formed in the same way as "reliable" are allowed to pass. To "demean oneself" in the sense of to compromise one's dignity, is housemaid's English; but is there any equivalent in English? I think we should be merciful to "demean."

The split infinitive is another crime for editors. I do not defend it, but I could quote many examples from our best prose-writers. "Ingenuity" is quite incorrectly formed, by a confusion of "ingenious" with "ingenuous"; but here protest would be useless. So we must admit morale as an English word, not printing it in italics. The French noun, for which we have no equivalent, is *moral*, which in English is an adjective. "Talented" I think is harmless, though it was once objected to.

But there are other much worse feats of journalese which often escape censure. "Meticulous" means timid. "Somewhat" is absurdly overworked. "Intrigued" in the sense of keenly interested is a quite unnecessary innovation. "Of that ilk" means "of that same"; "Rattray of that ilk" is another way of saying "Rattray of Rattray"; when the pedigree is in Latin it appears as *de eodem*.

Worst of all is the misuse of the word "hectic," dear to young ladies, who declare that they have had a hectic time. Hectic means habitual, permanent, and can mean nothing else. It is a medical term: a "hectic flush" is one which does not come and go; it is a usual symptom in the later stages of consumption.

Misunderstood medical words are rather common. For example, "recrudescence," which means renewed inflammation, or a fresh outbreak of an epidemic, is often used most inappropriately.

The doctors themselves are responsible for misspelling "aneurysm," which means the "dilatation" of an artery; "aneurism" could only mean absence of nerves or sinews. They have fortunately given up turning the good old English word "rickets" into "rachitis," which would mean inflammation of the spine.

The affected preference for Teutonic words has gone out since 1914, but I am still often asked to write a "foreword" to somebody else's book. I refuse even if it is called a preface, but more civilly.

If people must quote Latin, I wish they would do it correctly. *Cui bono?* does not mean, "What is the use?" but "Who profited by (the crime)?"

It was a maxim of a Roman lawyer named Cassius that if the author of a crime is unknown, the first question to ask is, Who gained by it?

Dementat in another favourite quotation is not a Latin word; and, in spite of Professor Huxley, *agnosco* does not mean "I am ignorant."

Our language is as well worth keeping in repair as our ancient buildings. It is as fine a tongue as any that is now spoken. It can express every idea and every mood. It is soft and pleasant to the ear, and yet peculiarly rich in short, vigorous, explosive sounds, which often seem exactly suited to the meanings which they convey. It is a heritage to be treasured and handed down unimpaired; and it will not take care of itself.

This is my advice to those who wish to write, and who wish as a matter of duty to acquire a good English style.

Steep yourselves in our best literature, and read aloud; this will prevent you from reading too fast. Write very slowly, taking as much pains as if you were learning to paint. Never, on any account, dictate. Do not imitate any particular author, but make it your object to say exactly what you mean, as simply, clearly and beautifully as you can. Be chary with your adjectives, and avoid all clichés like poison.

Put away your manuscript till you have forgotten it, and then correct it when you are in a captious frame of mind. Keep a notebook for ideas as they come to you, and write in it as carefully as if it was for publication. And remember that there are only two people whose good opinion you need care about—your Maker and yourself. They are both very hard to please.

III

EXAMINATIONS

On New Year's Day a conference opened in London, attended by a hundred professors, lecturers and secondary school teachers, to listen, at the first session, to a lecture by Sir Michael Sadler called "An Inquest on Examinations." He explained, however, that the corpse was not really dead. Sir Michael is also chairman of a committee which has issued a report called "An Examination of Examinations." I thought at first it was "An Examination of Examiners." That would be an exciting experiment indeed.

I will not discuss Sir Michael's, no doubt excellent, suggestions. But as I have done a good deal of teaching and examining in my day, I have formed some opinions on the subject of examinations and their influence upon education.

My subjects have been classics and divinity; I have had no experience with mathematics, science or history. To examine in the higher mathematics is a very highly skilled job, but I believe the merits of the candidates can be tested fairly accurately. It ought not to be very difficult to examine in history.

Bishops' chaplains do not find examinations for Holy Orders very satisfactory. The standard, even

306

now, is low, and a man may do a very good examination and be a very poor parish priest.

The old type of examination paper: "What do you know of Chedorlaomer, Chushanrishathaim, Mahershalalhashbaz, Huz, Buz, Luz and Uz?" is, I hope, extinct; but it is not easy to test the real fitness of a candidate. One young gentleman, asked to write out the Nicene Creed, declared, "I believe in all things, both visible and invisible." He thought that was quite safe!

In classics I think the examination system works fairly well. It encourages reading in masses (at any rate at Cambridge), and, for the sake of composition, close attention to style and literary beauty; further, a classical scholar must know at least as much of his own language as of Latin and Greek.

At Oxford every paper has to be independently read and marked by two examiners; a third is called in if differences of opinion may affect a man's class. The most difficult paper to mark is Latin prose.

The systems of marking at Oxford and at Cambridge are quite different. At Cambridge numerical marks are given and added up; the Oxford examiner is an impressionist; as he reads, a letter of the Greek alphabet forms itself in his mind.

The humours of examinations invade even the exalted seats of learning. At Brasenose the authorities once asked Pater, who was a Fellow, to examine the essays in a scholarship examination.

They thought the opinion of such a master of English style would be valuable. When they met, all that Pater said was, "O, I don't know. I thought them all very bad. There was one boy called Sanctuary. I liked his name!" He was not asked to examine again.

In a Fellowship examination the subject for the essay was Proudhon's "*La propriété, c'est le vol.*" A pessimist wrote on "Propriety is on the wing"; a paradoxical moralist on "Thieving is justifiable"; and a metaphysician on "Personality consists in volition." What were the examiners to do? French seems to lend itself to howlers. Who does not sympathize with the boy who, remembering a painful interview with the headmaster, translated "*Tout vient à point à qui sait attendre*," "Everything comes to a point to him whose seat is tender"?

In English literature I am inclined to think that examinations do more harm than good. Books about books about books! That is the way to prepare for an examination, but emphatically not the way to get all the good out of one of the noblest of all literatures. When the school of English was founded at Oxford, it was nearly killed by the philologists, who wished the candidates to learn Maeso-Gothic, Letto-Slavonic and Icelandic. These are subjects in which one really can examine! No doubt the subject is more rationally taught now, for it is very popular.

There must inevitably be some conflict between

education and examinations, because their aims are different. The object of education is not to help a boy to earn his living. It is, as Lord Bryce said, to stimulate curiosity, to help him to admire and love the right things. It is concerned with values, not with facts.

It aims at training the character through the intellect. "The intelligent man," says Plato, "will prize those studies which result in his soul getting soberness, righteousness and wisdom, and will less value the others." But examinations are intelligence tests, intended to pick out those who have acquired a certain kind of skill. The complaint often made is that these intelligence tests are not satisfactory, if they are to decide who is to get an appointment. Tests have been applied to schools which cater for different classes, and the children of well-to-do professional men come out better than those of the working-man. This result does not please everybody, and it is urged that the son of a lawyer or doctor has advantages at home which have not been considered sufficiently. This may be so; but heredity counts for a great deal. We do not expect a carthorse colt to win the Derby, nor the colt of a racehorse to drag a dray.

In choosing a career, there is an Institute of Industrial Psychology which claims to apply more practical tests than any examination. Perhaps employers may come to employ these experts in filling their vacancies.

On the whole, a system of mixed examination and nomination seems to work best. It has long been the method in the Indian Civil Service; and during the war the universities were invited to nominate men for commissions, a task which they discharged very well.

The real failure of our secondary and university education is in not making those who go through it permanently interested in the things of the mind. Too many men say, like Samuel Butler, "I don't say that I want to shake off the dust of my university from my shoes, but I do want to get some of it out of my eyes." And unlike Butler, they drop their intellectual interests altogether. This, however, is mainly their own fault. One man may lead a horse to the water, but twenty cannot make him drink.

SCIENCE

I

OUR POOR RELATIONS

I HAVE often wondered that philosophers and men of science are still to be found who maintain that there is a generic difference between the intelligence of human beings and that of the so-called lower animals. We are told that they have to be content with instinct, while we have specialized in intellect.

Descartes held that they are mere automata; no doubt it has been possible to maintain that we are only automata, "the most cunningly devised of nature's clocks," as I think Huxley put it.

This theory is perhaps rather out of date. The fact is that like other parvenus we are ashamed of our poor relations. Disraeli, unexpectedly appearing in gorgeous raiment at the Oxford Diocesan Conference while that body was discussing evolution, proclaimed that he was "on the side of the angels." Bishop Samuel Wilberforce, primed by Professor Owen, who was a really great anatomist, imprudently crossed swords with Huxley, and asked him whether he traced his descent from a monkey on the father's side or the mother's.

His attitude is still authoritative at Dayton, Tennessee (to be carefully distinguished from Dayton, Ohio). But the other day a small boy at the zoo, with a confused idea of the Birmingham controversy, said, "Mummy, have all these poor monkeys got to become bishops?"

It is odd that we should be so sensitive, for if we were so indelicate as to date our birth from our real beginning, we should have to acknowledge that we were once much lower in the biological scale than any mammal.

I have just been reading Köhler's famous book on *The Mentality of Apes*. Köhler spent several years in the company of chimpanzees at Teneriffe, making friends with them and observing their habits. He is described as now Professor of Philosophy at Berlin. I hope he will be careful, for are chimpanzees Aryans? At any rate, their noses are not Semitic.

There is a companion volume, by Zuckerman, about baboons. But baboons are not nice animals. "Manners they have none, and as for their customs, they are beastly." The chimpanzee, on the other hand, apart from his predilection for coprophagy (the obscurity of a learned language is here useful), is a gentleman. He has all the virtues and some of the faults of *homo sapiens*.

Köhler is mainly concerned to prove, as he does triumphantly, that the chimpanzee possesses real intelligence. He can carry out concerted plans. If he wants to draw food into his cage from a place out of his reach, he will fit a stick into a hollow bamboo, and will rake in the coveted morsel, always putting the end of the double stick beyond the object.

If the food is hanging from the ceiling, he will place one box on the top of another, or even make a pile of three boxes, and mounting on them will knock off his banana with a stick. But he will also take his man friend engagingly by the hand, and lead him under the banana, after which he will suddenly spring on his shoulder.

The little community invented games and then got tired of them, as humans do. One joke was to guide a procession of ants on to a stick, which they then licked clean. They started fashions, of which they also tired after a time. It became the fashion at different times to walk on their hind legs, to tear off each other's hair, like post-war young women, to carry rags, vegetables and flowers.

These acquired habits seem to me to be very important for naturalists, who are sometimes too much inclined to assume that there is no change or progress in animal societies.

Nothing surprised me more than to read that the apes at once recognized their own photographs. Like babies, they try to kiss their reflections in a mirror, and they were surprised to find that the photograph of a chimpanzee had no solid back to it. But the experiment with mirrors and photographs had a ludicrous consequence. The apes became so fond of their counterfeit presentments that they developed a Narcissus complex. They

315

were found gazing at their reflections in water or on any bright surface.

They look after each other kindly and efficiently when one of them is ill or hurt. Köhler once got a splinter into his finger, and showed it to one of his friends. The ape at once assumed the gravity and importance of a surgeon; he examined the wound, seized the hand and forced out the splinter by two very skilful squeezes with his fingers, and then he examined the hand very closely and let it fall, satisfied with his work.

It is curious that they were terrified of toys which even remotely resembled some animal, and were still more horrified when their master came to them wearing an ugly mask. Köhler thinks, and I agree, that this is superstition, like our ancestors' fears of ghosts and demons.

When a dog bays at the moon, is he not in a very rudimentary way saying his prayers? We once had two collies, one of which died. I pretended to see him in the corner of the room, and talked to him. The other dog, which had never loved its companion, showed unmistakable signs of fear.

Köhler soon found that the chimpanzees differed as much in character and intelligence as human beings. They were very clannish, and gave a new-comer a very bad time. They also formed cliques: two of them would strike up a warm friendship.

Did Köhler try to teach them to understand German? It seems to me that experiments of this kind might have been valuable. Dogs are sometimes astonishingly quick at recognizing the meaning of human speech.

In a house where I was staying the other day the hostess remarked to my wife, "Toby must be washed to-morrow." The dog, who was lying on the hearth-rug, understood perfectly, and was much agitated. On the next morning he hid himself and could not be found.

Is it not a horrible thing that over a great part of Christendom the authorized teaching is that since animals have no souls we have no duties towards them? I was amused to see that a clerical friend had put up a cross over his dog's grave. But, upon my word, I think he was nearer the true spirit of Christianity than those who accept the doctrine I have just mentioned.

I know that St. Paul asked contemptuously, "Doth God take care of oxen?" I am sorry that he said so. But a greater than St. Paul told us that no sparrow falls to the ground without God. We men, the tyrants and bullies of our planet, have yet much to learn about our duties to our poor relations, who have as good a right to life and happiness as we have.

317

II

CAT AND DOG

We shall never know how many thousands of cats perished in the mysterious epidemic which swept over their tribe in the winter of 1935–6. If they had been dogs, the Chancellor of the Exchequer would have been perturbed by the loss of innumerable seven-and-sixpences. But there are none to mourn a cat except its owners. We are still grieving over the loss of a tortoiseshell kitten, the prettiest and most affectionate little animal that ever was.

The Egyptians paid divine honours to the cat. Thousands of mummified cats have been found; I believe they were sold as fertilizers. The Greeks for some reason did not keep them as pets; the word usually translated cat really means a weasel.

In the Middle Ages they were closely connected with witchcraft. Shakespeare was already familiar with the inexplicable horror which the harmless necessary cat inspires in some people, even in gallant soldiers like Lord Roberts. I never heard a psychological explanation of this aversion, which seems to run in families.

The cat figures in many proverbs. "A cat may look at a king," if she is interested in royalty. But when pussy-cat went to London to visit the Queen, she saw nothing but a little mouse under her chair

—an apologue, I have long thought, of the "practical man," who all his life sees only what he can make use of, and misses all the rest.

"Care killed the cat"; that I am sure it never did.

"The cat shuts her eyes when she steals cream." Wrong again; the cat is not at all ashamed of her sins.

I wonder whether that most amusing little book, called *Very Original English*, is still remembered. It consists of authentic little essays by children at a primary school. The essay on cats is a masterpiece. "The cat is a quadruped, the legs as usual being at the four corners. . . . Do not tease cats, for, firstly, it is wrong so to do, and, second, cats have claws, which are longer than people think. Cats have nine lives, but which are seldom required in this country, because of Christianity."

The nine lives may perhaps be nine ways of escaping. But there is an old proverb that "the fox knows many tricks, the cat one," namely, to run up a tree. The original Greek proverb has a hedgehog in place of a cat; the "one good trick" of the hedgehog is to roll itself up in a ball.

A North Country farmer summed up the characters of his animals as follows: "You see, cats look down upon you, dogs look up to you, but pigs is equals."

He is right about cats and dogs. The verdict is amplified in a charming little poem by Sir William

Watson, that excellent poet who was allowed to grow old in poverty. He describes a walk with a highly bred dog, "the flower of collie aristocracy." "His salon manners, his society smile" were but skin deep; he had the instincts of a sheep dog; but "ancestral energy and strenuousness, in graceful trifling (were) frittered all away."

Then when they come home they find a great Angora cat, "throned in monumental calm, herself immobile, imperturbable." "She seemed the Orient spirit incarnate, lost in contemplation of the Western soul." "Even so, methought, the genius of the East, reposeful, patient, undemonstrative, luxurious, enigmatically sage, dispassionately cruel, might look down on all the fever of the Occident."

Cats do not shine in intelligence tests. They have not the slightest wish to satisfy the examiners, and never put themselves out. So it is no wonder that the authorities bring them out inferior not only to the anthropoid apes and elephants, but to dogs, beavers, horses, sea-lions and bears.

Cats do not care for human approbation. If they feel affection—and they often do—they will show it with a graceful air of conferring a favour; but they have not the slightest notion of obedience. They can do wonderful things in climbing and jumping; but if you try to make them show off they blandly refuse. They will not degrade themselves to be performing animals.

It is said that the Siamese cats are more responsive; but what are Siamese cats? The only occasion on which the B.B.C. announcer is recorded to have laughed was when he had to announce "Prince Damrong of Siam informs us that there are no Siamese cats in Siam."

So a Dalmatian gentleman showed me two Dalmatian hounds, and said to me: "I bought these in England; there are no Dalmatians in Dalmatia."

A queer story comes from the same country as my Dalmatian friend. A Jugoslav farmer, hearing a pitiable mewing in his farmyard, was just in time to see his cat carried off in an eagle's claws. Naturally he never expected to see his cat again. But three days later Pussy reappeared, limping and looking very uncomfortable. She was presently violently sick, and there was no mistaking what she disgorged. It was the indigestible portion of an eaglet! The feelings of the eagle when he returned to his eyrie may be imagined.

This rather tall story was told me in Jugoslavia, and I think it is probably true.

It is sometimes said that animal-lovers are those who have no human friends. I do not think it is true, and if it is, it is pathetic and not a reproach. There are stores both of intelligence and affection in many animals which we seldom take the trouble to explore. It is perhaps the strongest instance in which scientific discovery has revealed new moral duties.

Cats perhaps have not much heart. No cat would

do what my son's Alsatian hound did in Rhodesia, when he gave his life to save his master from being mauled by an infuriated baboon. My boy thought he was in imminent danger, and that the dog really saved his life; he flew at the baboon's throat, and the two animals rolled over dead together.

But a cat can be trusted to purr when she is pleased, which is more than can be said for all human beings.

III

TELEPATHY AND FAITH-HEALING

I HAVE been reading Upton Sinclair's book, *What God Means to Me*. Most of my readers know that Upton Sinclair is a novelist who has exposed the abuses of American big business with great vigour and bitterness, and who was defeated in an election campaign in California last year. He stood as what the Americans call a Radical, which in that country means not an advanced Liberal, but an extreme Socialist.

I am not concerned either with Mr. Sinclair's religion or his politics. But he confesses himself a reluctant convert to various beliefs which all my prejudices reject as mere superstitions.

His wife was cured by Christian Science, and so was he himself, when he was almost dying of "triple hiccuping." Coué has "helped him through many trials." He knows of seemingly miraculous cures in Mongolia, Mexico, Africa, China, Arabia, and at Lourdes.

He is much impressed by the case of Kuda Bux, a young Indian, who walked barefoot over a fire in two trenches eleven feet long and six feet wide, the surface heat of which was found to be 800 degrees Fahrenheit. Two medical students who tried

323

to emulate the feat were severely burnt and had to jump to safety.

This case is certified by the director of the surgical unit of St. Mary's Hospital, London, who witnessed the tests, which took place in a private garden at Carshalton. Sinclair also refers to W. J. Dunne's book about predictions of the future in dreams.

Mr. Sinclair and his wife have made experiments in telepathy and clairvoyance, which they claim to have proved. On the same day on which I read Sinclair's book I found in the *Hibbert Journal* an article on telepathy by Professor Joad, which adds fuller and more precise evidence to the results of Sinclair's experiments.

The first remark that occurs to me is that these alleged mysterious phenomena are not all of the same kind.

To take first cases of seemingly miraculous healing. I have given some attention to the subject, being a member of a committee of doctors and clergymen appointed by the late Archbishop Davidson.

It was very difficult to get trustworthy evidence, and as far as I know nothing was proved which the doctors were unable to account for, after allowing for the admitted effect of suggestion in functional disorders.

But it is not easy to draw a hard and fast line between functional and organic; Upton Sinclair mentions a case at Lourdes, certified by a great medical authority, of the cure of an ulcer of nine years' standing.

Of course the Virgin Mary had no more to do with this cure than Queen Cleopatra; but the name of Cleopatra would not have cured the patient. The cures, whether at Lourdes or in Mongolia, are wrought by suggestion; but it is essential to suggest to the patient that there has been no suggestion.

This the Christian Science healers know well.

I have been even more impressed by authenticated cases of faith-killing than of faith-healing.

An athletic young Maori accidentally ate some food reserved for his chief. He was not afraid of the anger of the chief; but the violation of the tabu filled him with such horror that he died in a few hours.

Sir Ernest Budge told me of a case at Khartoum. A native stole some money entrusted to him, and swore before the Kadi that he was innocent. The Kadi said that he must decide the case by ordeal. The litigants were made to drink some water into which writing from the Koran had been dipped; "Whichever of you is perjured," the Kadi said, "the wrath of Allah will fall upon him." The thief, after drinking the water, fell dead. An accusation of poisoning was referred to the pundits at Cairo, who after a careful inquiry reported unanimously that the man had died by the act of God.

It is plain that the whole subject needs much more investigation on strictly scientific lines.

There remain the alleged phenomena of clairvoyance and telepathy. Experiments have been carried on at Duke University, U.S.A., for three years; they have consisted chiefly in naming cards. The advantage of this method is that a mathematician can calculate the chances of correct guesses with great accuracy. If the proportion of correct guesses very largely exceeds the number which could be accounted for on a purely chance basis, we are almost obliged to admit that telepathy or clairvoyance has been proved.

"In the course of 2,250 witnessed trials, a subject called 869 cards correctly. This is 419 above the chance figure." "More sensational were telepathic experiments in which the persons were 250 miles apart; they managed to communicate with each other to the tune of an average of 10·1 correct calls per 25 cards."

Is it possible to escape from the perhaps unwelcome conclusion that these phenomena are genuine?

Chance may be ruled out at once. But how about fraud? Mr. Sludge the medium has had many followers. But is it likely that half a dozen members of a university staff would have wasted three years in monotonous experiments with the object of fooling each other and the public?

I am such a hard-boiled sceptic that I am only shaken, not convinced.

But if the evidence is really overwhelming, what does it mean? This is the question which Professor Joad tries to answer.

Is the development of life a passive process, as the materialists think, or is life always trying to insinuate itself through the crevices in the armour of matter? Is life striving to achieve a fuller and more intense consciousness? Each new achievement, once secured, passes into the instinctive, habitual, unconscious. Vital energy is then set free for further gains.

Is it possible that extra-sensory perception is a new faculty, appearing at present fitfully and sporadically, but beginning to establish itself? At present it is rare and unaccountable and easily put out of order. But it may be the latest product of evolution, the premonition of a new vital faculty. Perhaps some day we may rise "out of the realm of sensory experience altogether. We may proceed to the exploration of the universe without the aid of the senses."

Do I believe this? No, I really cannot.

I am not at all sure that our species is progressing, except as the result of accumulating knowledge.

But these mathematical tests at Duke University are very difficult to get over, and I can hardly justify my incredulity.

ENGLAND

I

THE LONDON JUMBLE

IT is interesting to compare Cohen Portheim's new book, *The Spirit of London*, with Paul Morand's *Londres*, which appeared a short time ago. The Frenchman's book is lively, witty and often acute; but the French never really understand England; perhaps they never understand any country except their own. They seem to be constitutionally unable to spell English words and names. We may remember Victor Hugo's wonderful "Lord Clanchailie," with his "bugpipc," his "philaberg," and his "smushingsmull."

Nor is it easy to explain how a man who was attached to the French Embassy for years can suppose that London is in a state of perpetual fog. If he did think so, he need not have said it nineteen times in three hundred pages; it becomes irritating.

Cohen Portheim, on the contrary, is almost never at fault. No born Cockney knows his London better than he did. His book is one of the best of guidebooks, though it is something better than a guidebook.

The premature death of this Austrian Jew was a calamity. His life's work was to help the nations of Europe to understand and respect each other, and especially to make England no longer "the unknown isle" to Continentals.

He liked and admired us sincerely, and was convinced that if Europe is to recover from its attempted suicide, as he calls it, in the Great War, our country must take the leading part in recalling it to its better self. Our national character and traditions, and even our geographical position and overseas interests, fit us, he thinks, to be the leaders in a new Europeanism.

For this is what he most desired. Why should not the nations of Europe, which share the same civilization, be good neighbours? Why should they not be good Europeans, as the inhabitants of the United States, drawn from every nation under heaven, are good Americans, and as the people of Switzerland, who speak three languages and profess two religions, are good Swiss? He would like to see a real European league, like the British Commonwealth of Nations. Failing this, Europe will attempt suicide again, and next time it will succeed.

His other message is equally important. Europe must stand for quality, not quantity. It is the vulgar worship of mere quantity, of huge figures, of "records," of mass-production and mechanical standardization, which is corrupting our social life. We begin to think we have followed false gods; for when "Success" fails, what is there left?

Looking at London, he sees ocular proof that the

Englishman is hopeless as a Communist. Our capital is unplanned; it is so chaotic that in spite of its size it is no more overwhelming than a long string of villages. We had a grand chance, after the Great Fire, of laying it out as the Americans, under French advice, laid out Washington. Wren wanted to do it, but we would not. And by the way, all lovers of London ought to know Brewer's drawings of the old city. In the sixteenth century it was one of the loveliest cities of the world, finer even than Oxford.

Again, we might have turned the Thames into a Grand Canal; but the Surrey side as it is does not remind us of Venice. We have stuck the Marble Arch in a ridiculous position. We have a conspicuous column with a gentleman on the top said to be a former Duke of York. Who was he and what did he do? Nobody knows or cares.

Triumphal arches and columns do not go well with a sense of humour; we cannot take ourselves so seriously as the old Romans. Our sense of humour certainly takes odd forms. We have a statue to Boadicea, who burnt London and massacred all the inhabitants, and a pygmy effigy of that disastrously successful rebel, General Washington.

We cannot swagger solemnly; our pageants are mixed with buffoonery, like the Lord Mayor's Show. London's tutelary gods are Gog and Magog.

Both of our observers note the unostentatious fronts of houses in the rich quarters. The palaces are few and by continental standards small. There are no flats with dining-rooms to seat a hundred as in the Tiergarten at Berlin.

The square miles of cottages in the East End are of course quite peculiar to England, and very characteristic. Our people like to have little homes of their own. On the Continent, where such houses are unknown, the advantages of our plan are beginning to be realized.

Both also notice, very truly, that the Englishman is not by nature or preference a townsman. The only people who know London and do not like it are a large proportion of Londoners. The foreigner dislikes it at first—we do nothing to make him welcome; but when he has made friends in London he is very happy there. Not so the Londoner, who rushes away at the week-end to some suburban or rural retreat; although no capital has such spacious parks—real parks, too, not laid out formally. But we are nearly all countrymen at heart.

I end with this little story. An ambassador from the sunny south, newly accredited to the Court of St. James's, asked a colleague whether it was pleasant to live in London, in our grim climate. "Yes," said the older diplomat, "I like London, and I like the English." "Why do you like them?" "Well, this people is not envious, not jealous."

That is true, and it means much. With all our faults, we are a kindly, good-natured people, with short memories for injuries. Our minds may

334

be as illogical as our huge jumble of a capital. But we have a deep conviction that the only irreparable mistakes are those which are made by consistent logicians. There is a kind of higher stupidity of which we are seldom guilty.

Foreigners think we are diabolically clever, under a mask of childishness. We are not clever at all, but it is true that we never quite grow up. Life for us is a kind of football-match, played according to the rules.

ST. GEORGE FOR ENGLAND

GIBBON has never been forgiven for grossly libelling our patron saint.

He identifies him with George of Cappadocia, the Arian Bishop of Alexandria from 356 to 361.

This George was born in a fuller's shop, and began his career as an army contractor. He supplied the Roman army with bad pork, and made his fortune. This did not prevent him from being made Bishop of Alexandria in place of the rightful bishop, Athanasius, who had been turned out.

As bishop he resumed his profiteering habits, which made him unpopular; and when Julian the Apostate restored the hopes of the pagans, they seized Bishop George and literally tore him limb from limb.

His unorthodox opinions prevented him from being canonized as a martyr.

This disreputable person is not the patron saint of England.

The authentic George was a "military tribune" —that is to say, a colonel in the Roman army, who was martyred during the last persecution, in 303, and buried at Lydda, where a sixth-century church erected in his honour still stands.

For some unknown reason he was called "the

336

great martyr," and legends soon gathered round his name. He was provided with a dragon as early as the sixth century, and with a horse in the thirteenth, after the Fourth Crusade. The horse in his statue at Constantinople, in the imperial palace, used to neigh violently when a hostile army approached the city.

He was adopted as patron saint of England by the Normans in recognition of the assistance which he gave to the Crusaders by appearing among them hurling javelins at the Paynims. In the fourteenth century the Order of the Garter was placed under his patronage, and his feast became a red-letter day in the Church Calendar.

I have not heard that he helped us in any of the battles on the Western Front. Perhaps he felt that his equipment was rather out of date. So much for St. George.

Are we really a patriotic people? Foreigners think we are.

During the war the Germans were fond of saying that the Englishman's motto is, "My country, right or wrong." This precious epigram was spoken by an American as a toast given at Norfolk, Virginia, in the year after Waterloo by a gentleman of the curious name of Decatur. I do not think it is true of our countrymen that they will defend their country's actions with a bad conscience.

We are not so demonstratively patriotic as most other nations.

We have an unusually large number of anti-patriots who, more or less sincerely, believe that England differs from other misguided rascals in never being in the right, even by accident.

But there is another reason. In Rudyard Kipling's *Stalky and Co.* there is a scene where a well-meaning visitor tries to rouse enthusiasm among the boys by flamboyant talk about "our country." It fell absolutely flat. That kind of thing, the boys thought, is in bad taste.

Again, a good deal of patriotism consists in hatred of other nations. We, I am thankful to say, are bad haters. We were worked up into hating Germany during the war, and we proved that Lowell's words about the national character are still true. "The Englishman is not quarrelsome, but he has an indefatigable durability of fight in him."

That we have short memories is illustrated by the following story:

An American and an Englishman met casually and got on very well together. When they parted the American said. "Well, sir, I like you very well; but I must tell you that I hate the English. I can't get over the burning of Washington." (This unfortunate incident took place in 1812. As an act of reprisal, our troops burnt some public buildings in the American capital.)

"No. Did we?" said the Englishman in surprise.

"Yes, you did."

"Well, that is really disgraceful. I knew we burnt

338

Joan of Arc, but I thought Washington died in his bed!"

The charge that we are arrogant and think ourselves superior to other nations is not true now, but I am afraid it was.

Even Froissart says that "Englishmen are so proud that they set no store by any nation except their own"; Michelet found in England "pride personified in a people"; and Mark Twain said, "The English are mentioned in the Bible; the meek-spirited shall possess the earth."

I fear the charge was true, and not so very long ago.

I sometimes refresh myself with the old volumes of *Punch*. I have the whole series, from 1841, and very good reading they are. But the cartoons from 1850 to 1870, including the American Civil War, really make one squirm. We are being whipped for our grandparents' transgressions.

This Palmerstonian swagger is quite different from the legitimate and proper pride which Queen Elizabeth, then old and feeble, expressed when Denmark offered to mediate between England and Spain. "I would have the King of Denmark, and all princes, know that England hath no need to crave peace; nor myself endured one hour's fear since I attained the crown thereof, being guarded with so valiant and faithful subjects."

There are two great forces struggling for supremacy in our world—nationalism and internation-

339

alism. Just now, nationalism is in the ascendant, and in some countries it is taking very ugly forms.

Some of our leading thinkers, like H. G. Wells, would like to abolish nationalism as an evil thing. Tolstoy thought the same. But many of those who refuse to love their country only desire a war of classes, a far more ignoble thing than romantic imperialism.

It was love of country which drew the rare tears from the eyes of Christ. It is a passion to be purified and ennobled, not destroyed.

In the great words of Abraham Lincoln: "With malice towards none; with charity for all; with firmness in the right as God gives us to see the right, let us strive on to finish the work we are in."

If the name of St. George means this to us, let us invoke him with all our hearts.

III

MILESTONES OF THE PAST

"I HAVE forgotten my Greek history. Who *was* Milestones?" someone asked when a popular play was produced which consisted, as most of us remember, of three scenes from social history, three chapters from the life of a nation, three stages in the evolution of a civilization.

The idea of a modern pageant in literary form was taken up by several novelists; among the most successful of such books are E. F. Benson's *As We Are*, Archibald Marshall's *Two Families*, and Rose Macaulay's *Told by an Idiot*. It is an excellent theme, combining, like life itself, tragedy, comedy and melodrama.

Melodrama is always a great part of human life. There is tragedy in the decay of a social system which, with all its faults, had great achievements to its credit, in the ruin and disappearance of old families, and in the disappointment of many hopes, the discrediting of many ideals, the failure of many prophecies. There is comedy in the changes of fashion, when the dictates of anonymous arbiters condemn to ridicule modes of dress and tricks of manner which only lately were copied with obsequious deference.

The old volumes of *Punch* give in a different form a

continuous pageant of English civilization from the beginning of the Victorian Age. The corn laws and the "big loaf"; Chartism (fomented, according to Mr. Punch, by French agitators); the jolly, arrogant generation of Palmerston, when we cheerfully insulted every foreign nation in turn; our inexhaustible patience in trying to satisfy the Irish; the familiar complaints of the "fast" "girl of the period," who was not very unlike the post-war "flapper," though those who only knew the skittish Flora as Aunt Florrie of formidable memory can hardly believe it; the rather snobbish jokes about "servantgirlism"; and Du Maurier's families of seven children all under twelve. The Empire, as we can now see, culminated at the end of the century; since then we have been struggling, not very successfully, to keep our position.

I was amused at myself to find that I liked the second act of *Milestones* the best. It gave us the manners and customs of the 'eighties, my first decade after reaching what were then oddly called years of discretion.

At Eton we were not taught, in those days, that life has any problems to solve, but at Cambridge I found that "life is real, life is earnest." We were nothing if not earnest in the 'eighties. To be earnest you had to be a Liberal, a "robust" Liberal if possible. "It would be much pleasanter to be a Conservative," said the junior dean of my college to me. "But—". But of course so cultivated a man

342

could not belong to "the stupid party"; and besides, we have consciences. Mr. Gladstone stands for Righteousness, whereas Mr. Disraeli, though he once proclaimed himself, at the Oxford Diocesan Conference, "on the side of the angels," never convinced the Nonconformist conscience that his wings had even begun to sprout.

And then there was Robert Browning, who has "so much more grip" than Tennyson. We must have a Browning Society, under Professor Westcott, to study him; and if, as is likely, we come to a passage which we cannot understand, we must write to the poet himself, who will reply that if it ever had any meaning he has forgotten what it was.

But before the end of the 'eighties the most earnest among us began to think that Liberalism after all belonged to the 'seventies. A group of young men who had been reading Marx on *Capital* called themselves Fabians, after a Roman general who foiled Hannibal by keeping out of his way. A sound policy when "the flowing tide" is with you, and progress a law of nature. It was only necessary to say pompously, "It is coming," and to watch its irresistible approach.

The survivors of the group now talk of "liquidating" those who do not agree with them; but in those days they had not yet been to Russia.

Their opponents said that State capitalism would not work. Herbert Spencer, who saw more clearly, said that it might work, but that it would make the Government omnipotent. It would mean slavery, "and the slavery will not be mild." Speaking as a Liberal, and assuming that Liberalism stands for liberty and Toryism for authority, he called Socialism "the new Toryism." Some of our young Conservatives seem to be coming to the same conclusion.

In the Church of England, priests with very long tail coats were defying their bishops to send them to prison for illegal "ritualism." A party of young Oxford men were discovering that the Church of England suffers from "State-blindness," so they founded the Christian Social Union, to combat "sweating," and especially lead-poisoning. Scott Holland, who had grasped the secret of oratory, never to use one word where five will do, was eloquent on these subjects. "Settlements" were started in the East End.

"Settlement" was a great word in the 'eighties. "I hope I shall live to see you settled," my father would say, meaning that he wished me to marry. Then he would see about the "settlements."

Slumming was becoming fashionable. What the East-enders thought of the gushing, devout and honourable women who descended upon them is uncertain.

The early Victorian conventions were still very strong. It was at an earlier date when Thackeray's (or was it Trollope's?) publishers made him alter

344

"fat paunch" into "deep chest"; but in a country walk the "gentlemen" were still asked to get over stiles first, and to "remember Lot's wife."

A woman who was soon to have a baby was "believed to be in a certain condition," by the newspapers; and a bishop—a good bishop too—hurled *Jude the Obscure* out of the window of a railway carriage, and wrote to *The Times* to say that he had done it.

William Morris was beginning to struggle against the hideous furniture of the preceding decade; but drawing-rooms were still choked with chairs and tables, and the walls covered with pictures, great and small, interspersed with crockery and Japanese fans.

I have been tempted to linger wistfully by this particular milestone. Some of our ideas of fifty years ago are probably dead, others will come back as the pendulum swings. We were happier then, and much more hopeful, than we have been since the war; more hopeful than we are ever likely to be again.

I have often wished that I had been born half a century earlier, and I once said so to the wife of a territorial magnate, whom I expected to agree with me. "I don't," she said. "Think of all the state my husband and I would have had to keep up." Perhaps she was right in preferring the simple life; but I confess that I am more thankful to have lived through the 'eighties, absurd as they were

345

in many ways, than to be still alive in 1936. We never thought then that civilization was in danger; it seems to be in considerable danger now.

Max Beerbohm once drew a series of symbolic pictures of John Bull, getting fatter and fatter through the last century, then woefully deflated, and finally contemplating a large note of interrogation.

The road looks like ending in a quagmire.

IV

WHERE IN ENGLAND WOULD YOU LIVE?

IF you were free to live wherever you liked in England, which county would you choose? That is what my wife and I had to decide three years ago. We were limited in our choice, because we wanted to be near Oxford and not far from London, so we chose a quiet village in Berkshire, buried in trees, just under the Sinodun Hills, and looking out on the Chilterns and the Berkshire Downs. It suits us very well; but we half hankered after two other districts, the Cotswolds and Dorsetshire.

On the whole, I think the best part of England is what the Americans would call the middle south-west. I mean the group of counties including Worcester, Hereford, Somerset, Wilts, Gloucester and Dorset. Perhaps I ought to add Devon, a county which I do not know well.

The Isle of Wight has a great charm, which it may soon be in danger of losing. All the home counties are too near what Cobbett called the great wen—London. They are not real country, though in parts of them one may forget the town.

No doubt other parts of the country have their champions. Kent is rich in military and ecclesiastical architecture, and the eastern part of the county, except by the sea, is unspoilt.

The eastern counties are still really agricultural, and though much of them is as flat as a pancake, we used to hear at Cambridge that the sky is unusually fine, and the remark is not quite absurd.

This part of England has one advantage in common with the Cotswolds—its magnificent parish churches, built out of the profits of the wool industry. The Perpendicular church is peculiarly English, with its great windows designed to let in as much sunlight as possible, and in East Anglia we admire the exquisitely carved wooden roofs and screens.

Havelock Ellis says that the eastern counties have produced a larger number of great men than any other part of England, and Dickens that if you have a spite against an insurance company you should buy an annuity and go and live in Norfolk. But in spite of these advantages, added to a very low rainfall, I should not choose this district, parts of which look like an extension of Holland. There is something sinister about the sea, which every year shears off a new bit of coast from our poor little island.

My native county, Yorkshire, has some beautiful river valleys; but in the North of England one is too often reminded that in spite of the Gulf-stream we are in the latitude of Labrador, and the winter nights are appreciably longer. Nor was I tempted by the Lake District, in spite of its charm. A rainfall of eighty inches damps my enjoyment of scenery.

But the south-west has not only a more genial climate; it has infinite variety. Dorset has rolling downs, rich water-meadows and wide parklands.

Somerset is even more varied. There are the gentle Quantocks, where young Wordsworth and Coleridge talked and wrote. There are bolder hills about Exmoor and a unique gorge at Cheddar. Athelney and Glastonbury once rose as islands above extensive marshes, like Ely in the Fen country. Glastonbury Abbey has perished, but at Wells the cathedral, the palace, the deanery and the Vicar's Close are the most perfect group of ecclesiastical buildings in England, with a tiny town clustered round them.

In both counties one cannot walk far without coming upon some beautiful old country house, sometimes grand, like Montacute, sometimes of a modest manorial size.

In this part of England we can almost forget that these beauties belong to a state of society which is rapidly passing away. If our churches and country houses were destroyed, should we have very much to show to a visiting foreigner?

There is a dignity about stone which brick cannot match. Bath is one of the most beautiful towns in England, still breathing the calm and self-assured culture of the eighteenth century. And a proposal to drive an arterial road through it was only defeated with difficulty!

The beauty of stone is of course undeniable in the Cotswold country. The famous Cotswold houses are all built of the local stone; the distinctive style was discovered about the end of the fourteenth century. The stone-mullioned windows grouped in tiers beneath moulded dripstones, the gables, chimneys and occasional projecting bays make one of the most pleasing types of domestic architecture that I know; and I never saw anything quite like them on the Continent. Yes, we were much tempted by the Cotswolds, after spending four summer holidays in Gloucestershire.

Shrewsbury and Ludlow are two of the most beautiful towns in England, unknown to thousands who visit Chester; but the Midlands are too often in a state of cold sweat, more clammy even than our seats of learning.

But the truth must be told. For about seven months in the year rural England is delectable; one can hardly go wrong in choosing a home there. But in winter, whether in town or country, our beloved fatherland is a good place to live out of.

We can sympathize with the old Roman who wrote about our island: *"Caelum crebris nebulis et imbribus foedum"*—"the climate, with its fogs and rains, is *disgusting.*"

V

A GREAT DELIVERANCE

THE four years war which ended on November 11, 1918, differed in many respects from all earlier wars. The numbers engaged on both sides were enormously greater, and the total of men killed in action or died of wounds—about ten millions—exceeded all records. But the proportion of lives lost to men mobilized was not above the average, although the fighting was almost continuous, whereas in previous wars, down to the Napoleonic campaigns, there were perhaps two great battles in a year, and on the large majority of days the soldiers were not in immediate danger. The nerve-strain in the war of 1914–18 was almost infinitely greater.

We may wonder why the wars fought under earlier conditions were so destructive of life. The answer is that deaths from disease, which on the Western Front accounted for a quite insignificant fraction of casualties, were formerly much more numerous than deaths from wounds. This change altered the balance of danger as between officers and privates, since the latter in the earlier wars were less well cared for than their commanders. I have compared many rolls of honour, and the proportion of deaths is very uniformly one in five or five and a half for officers, and one in ten or eleven for privates. The officers paid a double toll.

A few figures will illustrate the enormous wastage from sickness in earlier wars. In the wars with France between 1793 and 1815, 6,663 British sailors were killed by the enemy, 13,621 were drowned or killed in shipwrecks and fires, and 72,102 died of sickness. In the British Army, in the same period, 25,569 died of wounds, 193,851 of disease. Of Napoleon's Grand Army, which invaded Russia in 1812, only a few thousand out of 600,000 returned. At Vilna 25,000 out of 30,000 prisoners died of typhus.

In the Crimean War we lost 4,602 men by wounds, 17,580 by disease. The French lost 20,240 by wounds, 75,375 by disease. In 1877 the Russians, who were fighting the Turks, lost 30,000 killed and 80,000 by disease. In the Boer War we lost 7,534 killed and 14,382 by disease. In the Russo-Japanese War, for the first time, the losses by sickness were much less than the numbers killed in action.

Mercenaries, so largely employed before the nineteenth century, were not usually eager to kill or be killed, but the civil population suffered horribly. Germany was half depopulated during the Thirty Years War. At the sack of Magdeburg 20,000 non-combatants were massacred. Besides this, 100,000 Protestants were put to death for their religion in the Netherlands in the reign of

Charles V. Genghiz Khan and Timour had a pleasing habit of erecting pyramids of skulls to mark the sites of the towns they captured.

But in the eighteenth century war was far more humane than it was before or is to-day; there were singularly few atrocities in the Napoleonic campaigns.

In these computations, I have taken no account of the pandemic of influenza in 1918, which destroyed about fourteen million lives, one hundred and twelve thousand in Great Britain. It is doubtful whether it had much connection with the war.

Another remarkable fact about the last war is that hardly any great reputations were made. We honoured our most capable commanders, but there are no Blenheims or Trafalgars or Waterloos, no Wellington tombs or Nelson Columns, to commemorate the heroes of the Great War. On the other hand, we have our war memorials in every town and village, not all of them very beautiful, but testifying to a nation's gratitude to the undistinguished multitude who bore the burden and heat of the day.

Which are the best war memorials? I do not re for the Cenotaph, the merits of which seem me purely negative; it has no taste, either bad good. The great memorial at Edinburgh is the tribute of a nation; I wish we had something like it. The Campo Santo at Winchester College is very beautiful; and I should like to say a word for

the simple monument in the market-place of
Wallingford, my post-town. The two lines:

> Pass not this stone in sorrow but in pride,
> And strive to live as nobly as they died

could not be surpassed for beauty and dignity.

There is another new feature. Where is the *miles
gloriosus*, the braggart captain, who loves to fight
his battles o'er again? We never meet him. Those
who came back from the war never talk about it.
We forget, when we meet middle-aged men in
the ordinary concerns of life, that they went through
the most horrible experiences, and risked their
lives for us all.

Occasionally one has a shock. I remember
dining with a peaceful professional man, a solicitor,
I think, and noticing that his dining-room poker
was a saw-bayonet, a ghastly weapon. "Yes,"
he said, "that was within a few feet of my stomach
when I shot the man who carried it." (A British
general officer assures me that these weapons were
meant to saw wood, not to lacerate wounds;
~ ᴵ must give the Germans the benefit of th
ᴊoubt.)

These men must think of the war sometim
What are their thoughts about it? Perhaps t
try to put it away like a bad dream; but it m
come back to them, by night or day. One thing I
have noticed. It is not in ex-Service-men that we
find bitter feelings against Germany. On the con-

trary, they have a sincere respect and even liking for their former enemies, a feeling which I believe is reciprocated by German officers and soldiers towards ourselves. Meetings of ex-Service-men, British and German, are always friendly.

Are we in danger of forgetting the lessons of the war? Do our young people know or care much about it? Do they realize what modern war means? It is not easy to answer these questions; but the continued resolve to make Armistice Day a holy day of remembrance is very remarkable. There was not the same feeling about Waterloo Day. It was remembered by old soldiers; but not so many years afterwards the mob chose June 18th to break the Duke of Wellington's windows. "An odd day to choose," said the Duke.

What are the thoughts of the vast crowds who stand bare-headed and silent at the top of Ludgate Hill, where I so often watched them from the west front of St. Paul's? It was the most moving sight I ever saw, and there is no sign that Londoners are beginning to feel that there is anything unreal about it.

There is certainly no exultation, still less any vindictiveness. There is, I think, a wish to thank God for a great deliverance, not for a victory. There is no wish that the war had been prolonged so as to see Germany invaded, and perhaps her capital occupied.

A great deliverance from a terrible danger,

355

and the wish to pay a reverent tribute to those who risked and those who gave their lives for our beloved country; that tremendous sacrifice which they never talk about themselves, and of which on ordinary days we are not sufficiently mindful. There is the wish to join in sympathy with the parents, wives, sweethearts, brothers, sisters and children for whom life can never be quite the same since a dearly loved member of the family yielded his gallant spirit on the fields of France.

And there is an earnest prayer, and a fixed determination, that if we can help it this horrible catastrophe shall never again bring ruin and misery upon nations bound together by a common religion, a common civilization and culture, and a hundred links which ought to make for friendship. "Sirs, ye are brethren; why do ye wrong one to another?"

VI

THE LANDED GENTRY

AFTER fifteen years, a new edition of Burke's *Landed Gentry* has appeared. It has cost an immense amount of labour, and is unfortunately incomplete, since many heads of families have grudged spending an hour or two in bringing their pedigrees up to date. But it is a valuable and interesting contribution to the social history of a country where there is no wall of partition between noble and commoner, and where the large class of plain gentlemen and ladies has been constantly augmented by families who have risen in the social scale. The upper middle class in Great Britain has no exact parallel on the Continent.

It is a pathetic volume, for it chronicles the inevitable decay of one of our institutions. Scores of old families were extinguished by the Great War. Many hundreds have been driven from house and home by the new methods of political corruption, infinitely more destructive than those of the bad old days, when politicians bribed honestly with their own money, and recouped themselves by jobbery! The landed class have been marked down for spoliation, and in fifty years there will not be many of them left.

I could not defend the continued existence of

a leisured caste, no longer able to justify their existence by the discharge of the numerous unpaid duties which formerly belonged to the landowner. The younger men of our day would not be unemployed country gentlemen if they could. People now live longer; and when the old squire drops off at eighty, his son may have become a competent colonel or stockbroker, but he is likely to have no taste for hunting, shooting and fishing, and no knowledge of estate-management. The old order is doomed, even without the help of the Chancellor of the Exchequer.

And yet it is difficult not to sigh when one visits an old village, lying round a charming group of the hall, a lovely Tudor or Georgian house, the church, to which each century has added something characteristic, and the rectory, where the squire's brother—not much of a priest, it is true—set a good example of clean living and unostentatious charity. The hall is now derelict; the "Old Rectory" has been sold to a retired professional man; the old life of the parish is gone.

Apart from futile regrets, what are our impressions in turning over the pages of this portly volume?

First, I think, we are struck by the extraordinary stability of English social life. Family after family has lived in the same place and much in the same way for three or four hundred years. An unexpectedly large number still "call their lands after their own names," or are called after the names of their lands; they are "of that ilk," as they say in Scotland.

For generation after generation the eldest son has been the squire, high sheriff of the county, a J.P., perhaps in Parliament. The younger sons have belonged to a strictly limited number of professions, of which the Church and the Army were the favourites. If the male line peters out, a son-in-law takes the family name and arms, and the succession is carried on.

There used to be a saying in the North of England, "Clogs to clogs in three generations." This is certainly not true of the landed gentry. If a family rises in the social scale, it stays there. This is why it used to be so well worth while, from the worldly point of view, to make a fortune. The family was "founded" on a secure basis for centuries to come.

Of course there have always been spendthrifts who have ruined themselves and their families by gambling (very prevalent in the eighteenth century) and horse-racing. Another expensive folly was building large houses, which the present owners are pulling down or selling for an old song. But in most cases the old family jogged along until the Great War, and the invention of the blessed word "Social Services."

Social satirists have amused themselves with stories of citizens who have taken aristocratic names. Poor Mr. Bugge may be pardoned for calling himself "Norfolk Howard," though he never heard the last of it. A Mr. Stubbs is said to have divided his name into "St. Ubbs." But I think the habit of taking Norman names was not common except in the reigns of George III and George IV. Then it was that Mr. Maude became Lord de Montalt, Mr. French Lord de Freyne, Mr. Basset Lord de Dunstanville, and the architect Wyatt blossomed out as Sir Jeffry Wyattville. Mr. Wilkins became de Winton, Mr. Hunt de Vere, Mr. Mullins de Moleyns, Mr. Morres de Montmorency. (My authority here is Mr. Ralph Dutton, in his charming book, *The English Country House*.)

To a student of eugenics perhaps the most interesting question is, How far has talent been transmitted in these families? I should say that there are very few examples of marked ability persisting in a family beyond the third generation.

There are a few famous families, like the Cecils and Churchills, in which there has been a revival of great mental powers after several generations of mediocrity; but in these cases the new ability probably came in as the result of a fortunate marriage.

There are, however, some surnames which an ambitious man might be glad to possess. Such are Pollock, Darwin, Coleridge, Haldane. In the Darwin family there have been five generations of very able men.

But on the whole, this volume does not lead us to attach much importance to "blue blood," apart from the very harmless form of snobbishness which makes a man mildly pleased to be one-five-hundredth Plantagenet.

I believe there are about 60,000 legitimate descendants of Edward III now living, and each of them may claim to be descended from King Alfred, Charlemagne and St. Louis of France. But who knows? As Dickens says, "Accidents will happen in the best regulated families."

From the eugenic point of view, there may be ten per cent of our population who are so well endowed physically, mentally and morally that they ought to have large families. There are probably another ten per cent who ought not to have children at all. But the remaining eighty per cent do not, I think, differ much in their chances of being desirable or undesirable parents. Political prejudice sometimes distorts our judgment in one direction or the other.

There is a reasonable kind of family pride, and I cannot understand how the inheritor of an honourable name—whether it be distinguished or not—can deliberately will its extinction by refusing to have children.

The old-fashioned large family is gone, and no sensible person wishes to revive it; but surely one of the chief happinesses of later life is to see one's children, and perhaps one's children's children, preparing to take their place in the world, and to keep alive those little family loyalties which have meant a good deal to ourselves.

VII

GENTLEMEN *v.* PLAYERS

WE English all love a half-timer. In our heart of hearts we regard life as a great game, to be played vigorously, fairly and good-temperedly, but not furiously, as if we thought that success in our chosen pursuit was the one thing in the world worth having, and that "all is fair in war." Whether we approve or not, this attitude is a national characteristic, which has impressed itself upon the whole of our social life.

The English statesman before the days of paid members and trade-union officials was always an amateur. Sometimes he was a sportsman, like Lord Rosebery, who said while he was a schoolboy that he had three ambitions—to win the Derby, to marry a millionairess, and to be Prime Minister. He did them all. Sometimes he was a *très grand seigneur*, like Derby, Devonshire and Salisbury.

These men were trusted, just because they had no axe to grind, and were slightly bored with politics. To yawn heavily while making a speech in Parliament would not be a recommendation in any other country.

Others among our leading statesmen have been scholars, historians or philosophers. The wholetime politician we dislike and distrust. If he quarrels with the soldier in time of war, we instinctively side with the soldier.

In religion, we prefer to listen to the layman. Who have been the most influential religious teachers in this country? First of all, the poets. The best English poetry has usually been moral or religious. We may think of Spenser, Milton, Tennyson, Browning and a multitude of lesser names.

Religious philosophy has been very influential in England. Coleridge, T. H. Green, Pringle-Pattison, Bernard Bosanquet, Clutton-Brock and others have moulded our thoughts on theology more than any clergyman. It is, I think, remarkable that even in the authoritarian Roman Catholic Church the ablest champions of the faith to-day in England are laymen—the late Baron von Hügel, Christopher Dawson and Alfred Noyes.

In philosophy we may make a more sweeping generalization. The living names—those whose books are read—are not systematizers but poets. Such are Plato, Goethe, Schopenhauer, Nietzsche.

History has usually been in the hands of non-professionals. From Thucydides the mine-owner (and unlucky admiral of the fleet) to Grote the banker and Acton the peer, the historian has generally been well-to-do and not immersed in his books. It is remarkable how well our statesmen have done in history—Macaulay, Rosebery, Winston Churchill. They have gained greatly by knowing politics from the inside, as Julius Caesar and Napier by knowing war from the inside.

The amateur has been equally prominent in English science. We have all heard the story of how an Englishman, a Frenchman and a German were see to write an essay about the camel. The Englishman visited the lands where camels live; the Frenchman spent an hour in the Jardin des Plantes, and produced a brilliant sketch, "Voilà le chameau"; the German went to his study and evolved the idea of a camel out of his inner consciousness.

The English amateur scientist has often been in a position to travel and see things for himself. Charles Darwin and Francis Galton are typical in this respect.

In economics the advantages of amateurism are not so apparent. Napoleon said that however firmly a constitution was based, the theories of economists could reduce it to powder. Napoleon hated all "idéologues," except in the art of war; but our parlour revolutionists, who know nothing of business, and divide their time between their study chairs and the platform, are enough to make one sick.

In medicine the average Englishman prefers the quack, especially if he buttresses himself with solid slabs of superstition. Here the advantage is all with the professionals and those who trust them.

364

In art the admired critics are mostly those who cannot paint, just as the educationists are those who cannot teach. In literature there used to be a slight tendency for writers to be half-ashamed of their craft. Congreve, the dramatist, disgusted Voltaire by saying that he wished to be treated as a gentleman, not as an author. But perhaps he only meant, "Please don't talk about my wretched books"—a remark which an Englishman might well make, and a Frenchman would not understand.

I suppose it is true that Scott was not proud of being a novelist; it was not quite the thing for the descendant of a long line of fighting Scotts. Rubens, on the other hand, snubbed a friend who found him painting and said, "So his Excellency the Ambassador amuses himself with painting." "On the contrary," said Rubens, "his Excellency the painter amuses himself with politics."

There is a growing resentment against the whole-time money-grubber. I have quoted already the obituary notice of Holloway (of the Pills). This is exactly the sort of thing which the Englishman dislikes. It is not playing fair. If a man likes to devote every day of his life to collecting postage stamps or walking-sticks, it is not worth while to lock him up; but the insatiable accumulator of stocks and shares is a public nuisance, who to the best of his ability makes our whole social order seem ridiculous.

But our love of the half-timer is perhaps most

in evidence in sport. We have been much exercised by the poor figure which our country cut in the recent Olympic Games at Berlin. Our athletes really did very well, but they were beaten nearly every time by men who had been trained like racehorses.

If we were not afraid of being called bad losers, a charge which we should resent vehemently, we should say what is really in all our minds. We have invented most of the good games. We have taught the world how to play them. And now we are beaten by people who do not understand that such things are not the main business of life. They take them in the wrong spirit, and spoil everything.

It is rather interesting that Euripides brings the same charge against the original Olympic Games. "Of all the countless evils in Greece, none is worse than the race of athletes." He attacks them exactly in the same way as Rudyard Kipling, with his "flannelled fools and muddied oafs."

Well, are we to approve of this characteristic of our countrymen or not? There are dangers in our mistrust of specialists, as I have hinted. But, on the whole, I think we are right. The whole-timer is not always a safe guide. Lord Salisbury once complained: "If you trust the doctors, nothing is wholesome; if you believe the theologians, nothing is innocent; if you believe the soldiers, nothing is safe."

He who will learn many trades shall be Jack of all, and he that will know only one trade shall know none.

We all have to specialize, and in doing so to go without many good things which we should like to know and to be; but we are sent into the world to be, as far as possible, complete and rational men and women. Intense concentration makes this impossible, and queers the pitch for our neighbours.

OTHER NATIONS

I

THE HEATHEN CHINEE

I DO not wonder at the immense success of the Chinese Art Exhibition. I came away from it full of astonishment and admiration and with certain other feelings.

Palmerston in the House of Commons spoke of the Chinese as "insolent barbarians," because they objected to having Indian opium forced upon them. To show our superior civilization we burnt the emperor's palace, full of irreplaceable art treasures.

In 1900 the Kaiser, addressing his marines about to start for China, adjured them as follows: "You are about to meet a crafty and cruel foe. Give no quarter!" The Allied contingents, except the British and Japanese, needed no exhortations to commit outrages. Many Chinese girls threw themselves into wells rather than fall into the hands of the Christians, and the destruction of art treasures was even greater than in 1860.

We called the Chinese insolent barbarians; they called Europeans foreign devils. Which name is best deserved?

Barbarians the Chinese are certainly not. Their art was at its best—so they think themselves—in what we call the Dark Ages, when Europe was a welter of savagery and cruelty. Their pottery and porcelain, their painting of plants, flowers and animals were far in advance of anything that Europe could produce.

It was no brief efflorescence of genius; their work has been beautiful, without a break, from the Christian era to quite recent times.

Admiration of China is not a new thing in Europe. There was a rage for everything that was believed to be Chinese in the eighteenth century.

Chippendale chairs are in the Chinese manner. A few faded Chinese wall-papers still hang on the walls of old houses. Willow-pattern plates, first designed in Shropshire, are supposed to be peculiarly Chinese.

Louis XIV appeared at a court ball in what he meant to be a Chinese costume. Louis XV, in imitation of Chinese custom, guided the plough in the early spring. We built a pagoda in Kew Gardens.

These compliments were returned. The Emperor of China built a model European village, and dressed his coolies as French peasants.

Unfortunately, the connoisseurs of the eighteenth century were completely though pardonably ignorant. Not for them the paintings of hawks and kites which frightened pigeons away, and the painted cats which were warranted to keep a house free from mice.

The wily Oriental sold to the Europeans things which he did not value, and manufactured them to suit Western taste. Soon the faker was at work.

372

"Of every ten Sung paintings," they say in China, "eleven are spurious."

We often hear that the Chinese anticipated nearly all our discoveries, from paper to gunpowder, but brought none of them to perfection. Whether they have really reached an era of stagnation, it is not easy to say.

But they suffered the greatest misfortune that can happen to any people; they were conquered by the Central Asiatic nomads, who, under the names of Huns, Mongols, Tartars and Turks, have wrecked civilizations from Hungary to the Pacific.

We have all heard amusing stories of Chinese manners and customs—their ceremonious politeness; their embarrassing questions, which have put to rout even an American interviewer; and their topsy-turvy customs, such as paying your doctor an annual sum so long as he keeps you in good health, and no longer.

We have heard of a Chinese host pinning a yellow patch on the dinner napkins, white being the mourning colour in China. And we are told that a Chinese executioner can cut off your head so neatly that until he asks you to bend forward you do not know that it is off.

No one who is interested in proverbial wisdom should neglect the proverbs which the Chinese love to introduce into conversation. Here are a few specimens:

373

No needle is sharp at both ends.

Do not remove a fly from your friend's forehead with a hatchet.

One dog barks at nothing; the rest bark at him.

He who rides on a tiger can never dismount. (For dictators.)

Free sitters grumble most at the play.

What will be the future of this remarkable people? At present they look like breaking up. But nothing hitherto has seriously shaken the stability of Chinese social life.

Dynasty follows dynasty; but the manner of life of the people changes very little. They have not been so ready as the Japanese to Westernize themselves, and from the military point of view they are weak; but those who know them have no illusions about their survival value. They can outwork and undersell even the Japanese; they can live in all climates from Siberia to Singapore.

Americans and Australians are convinced that the Chinese must be kept out at all costs; white labour cannot compete with them. When Chinese coolies were employed on the Rand, British Labour became violently excited about (so they said) the effect on the morals of the coolies!

We sometimes forget how recent and how precarious the ascendancy of the white races is. For a thousand years before the beginning of the modern period Europe had been on the defensive. Huns, Arabs Tartars and Turks—successive

374

waves of Asiatic conquerors—nearly submerged Christian civilization.

Only once before modern times did the West effectually turn the tables—when Alexander the Great, taking advantage of a temporary superiority in military science, led a Greek army across the Indus. Trajan, however, brought the Roman eagles to the Tigris.

Now, with the help of modern discoveries, the white man has conquered nearly the whole of the habitable globe. In 1914, out of the fifty-three million square miles which make up the land surface of the earth (excluding Antarctica), only six million were not under white control.

But the tide had already begun to turn, when in 1904 Japan challenged Russia and won, thus proving that an Asiatic army, with equally good weapons and training, may be a match for the same number of Europeans. A thrill went through the whole continent of Asia. It has not been and will not be forgotten.

But the competition with China will be economic, not military. The Chinese, as Lafcadio Hearn says, are "a people disciplined for thousands of years to the most untiring industry and the most self-denying thrift, under conditions which would mean worse than death for our working masses."

Will the final victory fall to the high standard races or to the low standard races?

That is a question which only the future can answer.

II

WE EUROPEANS

THREE well-known men of science—Julian Huxley,
A. C. Haddon and A. M. Carr-Saunders—have
joined in an energetic protest against political
ethnology, that science falsely so called which is
based on the idea of *race*, and which, with tragic
results, has been used to justify political ambitions
and social grudges.*

The nonsense talked on this subject, especially
in Germany, is enough to make any genuine
biologist see red.

Here is one specimen, not quoted in this book; it
is from *New Bases of Racial Research*, by Professor
Gauch. "In non-Nordics the teeth, corresponding
to the snout-like narrowness of the upper jaw,
stand at a more oblique angle. Nordics masticate
with the mouth closed; men of other races make a
smacking noise like animals. The bright red mouth
of Nordics attracts and provokes kisses; it is kiss-
capable. The non-Nordic's broad-lipped mouth,
with dilated nostrils, displays sensual eagerness,
with a false and malicious sneering expression.
The Nordic race alone can emit clear sounds:
those made by non-Nordics are like the noises
made by animals, barking, sniffing, snoring and

* *We Europeans*, Cape, 8s. 6d.

376

squeaking. If non-Nordics are more closely allied to monkeys than to Nordics, why cannot they mate with apes? The answer is that perhaps they can."

Our authors have no difficulty in proving that there is no pure Nordic race, even in Sweden, and certainly not in Germany. There are no pure races anywhere.

Even the Jews have been a mixed race since they first entered Palestine. They liked to believe that they exterminated the people of the land; but Ezekiel's words, "Thy mother was a Hittite and thy father an Amorite," let the cat out of the bag. At present, the Sephardim approach the Mediterranean type, the Ashkenazim are often like the northern Slavs. But the Jewish nose seems to be Hittite.

The nations of Europe are Nordic, Alpine and Mediterranean in different proportions, with infusions of sub-varieties called Dinaric and East-Baltic, and here and there a Mongolian strain.

A nation is a society united by a common fable as to its origin and a common antipathy to its neighbours. We are all chosen peoples in our own eyes.

France is "la tête du monde civilisé." Britain takes up the white man's burden, and "bears on shoulders immense, Atlantean, the load, wellnigh not to be borne, of the too vast orb of her fate." The United States is God's own country. Germany has her "good old ally, God," whose personal name is

377

certainly not Jehovah, and may be Odin. And so with all the other nations, including China, which divides mankind into Chinese and "foreign devils."

But it is one thing to prove that in point of fact there are no pure races and another to argue that race does not matter.

This book does not hang together very well. The writer of the preface, who I have no doubt is Julian Huxley (since I heard him express similar sentiments at the annual Eugenics dinner), thinks that biological factors are less important than social problems. In other words, he wants to leave eugenics alone till we have had a socialistic revolution.

Haddon, who is probably responsible for the very able ethnological chapters, would not, I think, agree; nor should I. It is interesting to contrast the influence of careful pedigree-study on the betting for the Derby with our reckless indifference to heredity in human beings. So far from putting eugenics aside till a more convenient season, I am convinced that there is no time to lose. Counter-selection is going on rapidly and unchecked.

There is reason to believe that when a mixed race settles down without much further foreign admixture a very distinctive type emerges. The strongest example is that of the ancient Greeks, who seem to have been a very happy mixture of predominantly northern invaders and Mediterranean natives.

The portrait busts of eminent Greeks are not all authentic, and very few are contemporary; but the type, the finest ever known, was a real one. It disappeared gradually when new streams of broad-headed immigrants came into Greece; Cicero was much disappointed with the looks of Greek boys.

I have often noticed that the Roman portrait busts, evidently admirable likenesses, are not at all like modern Italians, but are rather like modern Englishmen. The Roman ladies especially have a very English look. But I have no explanation to suggest.

The Jews have also developed a marked type of their own, and so I think have the Lowland Scotch, though their racial composition is the same as that of Northern England.

This theory, if it is correct, would suggest that our authors have gone too far in discrediting the idea of race altogether. They have ingeniously supported their case by printing sixteen photographs of men of different nationalities and challenging their readers to guess where they come from. The portraits seem to have been chosen so as to give no indications of nationality. I confess that I guessed only one right—the Italian—out of fifteen; the sixteenth, Ambassador Sthamer, I knew personally.

I suggest that a much fairer test than that offered by the authors of *We Europeans* would be to take six or eight or ten portraits of representative men

379

in Britain, France, Germany and Italy and to see whether they exhibit such marked characteristics that any good judge who did not identify the subjects could place each portrait in one of four heaps and make very few mistakes. This would be a very different result from the guessing game in which I failed so signally.

For Germany we might take Luther, Haeckel, Helmholtz, Wagner, Bismarck, Mommsen, Schopenhauer, Moltke, Hindenburg and Ludendorff. I do not think there would be many mistakes with any of these.

For France we might take Richelieu, Fleury, Renan, Anatole France, Clemenceau, Foch, Poincaré.

For Italy, Machiavelli, Savonarola, Raphael, da Vinci, the Doge Loredan, with other famous portraits of Italians, Napoleon and Mussolini.

For our own country, could anyone mistake for other than a Briton Samuel Johnson, or Palmerston, or Melbourne, or Gladstone, or Hartington, or Salisbury, or Tennyson, Dickens, Matthew Arnold, Darwin, Herbert Spencer?

Nevertheless, three-quarters of what is written about national character is nonsense, as we realize when we read what other nations say of us. We are told that "England is the country of *will*"—we really take life rather easily. "The English are a nation of shopkeepers"—we are not close-fisted enough to be good shopkeepers. "England may be summed up as Beer and Bible"—we are a temperate people, and I regret to say we do not read our Bibles. "The English are so melancholy that they often commit suicide"—our suicide rate is one of the lowest in Europe.

Our foreign critics, moreover, do not agree; I cannot remember any quality that I have not heard attributed to my countrymen, except meekness and loquacity.

III

SPAIN

AFRICA, say the French, begins at the Pyrenees. This range is much more of a barrier than the Alps. North of it is a garden; south of it a brown, sun-baked country—desert and oasis, scrub-land and steppe. Under the fierce sun everything is black or white; there are no gradations and no half-lights.

It is African, too, in another way. In spite of the early settlements in the Peninsula of Celts and Goths, the basis of the population is Iberian, the race which ethnologists call Mediterranean, the short, long-headed, dark race which came to Europe from North Africa.

The Carthaginians, who planted factories in Spain, were partly of this race, not pure Phœnicians; and the Moors, though they used negro troops to help them in their conquest of Spain, were themselves Berbers, no darker in complexion than the Spaniards themselves, and racially akin to them. Othello was not a black man.

The mingled fire and ice of this strange land seems to have passed into the character of the people, especially if we regard the Castilian as the typical Spaniard.

But even in cruising round the coast-towns one

is struck by the great differences between the Galicians, who are half Portuguese, the indolent Andalusians, and the defiantly independent Catalans, who often shout "Down with Spain." Physically, the Spanish are more one race than the French; but France is united, one in sympathy and civilization; Spain is not.

Ever since the sixteenth century, when the Spanish infantry was the terror of Europe, that country has been strangely cut off from the rest of the Continent. Spanish power collapsed rather than decayed after the reign of Philip II.

"Spain makes men and wastes them," was a proverb. They were wasted in incessant wars; they were scattered over the vast spaces of Spanish America; they were sterilized by clerical celibacy (as late as 1750 there was one priest to every thirty inhabitants), and decimated by the Inquisition, which raged impartially against Moslems, Jews and heretics.

The Renaissance meant nothing in Spain; there was no Reformation; no revolution of the French type. Spain skipped the nineteenth century with its industrialism and liberalism altogether; and in the Great War both sides almost forgot that Spain existed.

Until lately, the power and wealth of the Church seemed to the stranger to be overwhelming. A Spanish bishop had the grand air of an eighteenth-century duke.

Those who wish to know what the life of a Spanish cathedral close was like forty or fifty years ago should read *The Shadow of the Cathedral*, by Blasco Ibañez; it has been translated. Ibañez is a bitter anti-clerical; but the description of Toledo Cathedral, with its six hundred officers and servants of all grades, is thrillingly interesting. Fifty years ago an Englishman in Spain was pointed at as "a heretic," not with animosity, but as we might say, "There goes a Chinaman."

And yet the lack of reverence is amazing. One might see a dog curled up in the episcopal throne in the sanctuary, or a cat receiving the caresses of the worshippers at mass.

The list of notices which I saw on the cathedral door at Cadiz was instructive. Young men were not to stand at the door staring at the women; this was not obeyed, but to stare at a lady is a compliment in Spain. Spitting, etc. (the Spanish language seems to be rich in words for these habits), was forbidden; and "the dog is not in his right place in the house of God." At Toledo there is an official called "el perrero" to drive dogs out. But, after all, "Paul's walk" before the Great Fire was rather worse.

The Spaniards are indignant when they are called cruel. Perhaps some other word might be found; but there is in the Spanish character a gloomy fascination for blood, pain and death, which is very apparent in their art. Perhaps a nation which

384

a hundred years ago enjoyed bull-baiting and cock-fighting cannot afford to throw stones at the bull-ring, which, they say, is now rather less brutal; but with us these cruel sports were never national institutions.

As for the Inquisition, we are told that torture was applied every day in the secular courts, and that the methods of torture employed by the Church were, if anything, less atrocious than those sanctioned by the State. Well: let anyone read Lea's *History of the Inquisition* and make the most of any excuses which occur to him. In war the Spaniards have always been cruel; the only great atrocities during the Napoleonic wars were committed by the Spanish guerillas and by the French in retaliation.

I fear we cannot acquit this people of a kind of savagery; even the Spanish mystics seem to revel in torture, directed, in their case, against themselves.

All travellers in Spain are charmed by the total absence of vulgarity and snobbishness. Poverty is not a thing to be ashamed of; every Spaniard is a gentleman, and expects to be treated like one. When an Englishman repulsed a beggar, he was rebuked with, "Perhaps the señor did not understand; the caballero was asking for money!" But the priests and monks are frequently insulted in the streets, for the Church is hated by a large section of the population.

Is this last fortress of medieval splendour and romance to be destroyed? Must we see the grand monuments of florid Spanish Gothic, those huge and sombre churches, burnt or desecrated? Even those who are aware of the many sins of the Catholic Church in Spain must hope that such a disaster may be averted.

Lenin, who in his satanic way was a shrewd observer, predicted that the first European country to follow Russia in a red revolution would be Spain. These two nations, at the opposite extremities of the Continent, resembled each other in several ways. Both were illiterate; both had remained untouched by the great movements of modern civilization; both were burdened with a rich and obscurantist Church; and in both the differences between rich and poor were very great.

In Andalusia especially, a province where the estates are large, the peasants were always half-starved. Above all, the middle class, which makes links between rich and poor, and is always a stabilizing element, was very weak both in Russia and Spain. Lenin's prophecy has unhappily come true.

And yet it is most unlikely that the outcome of the troubles will be Bolshevism. For the Spaniard is the most sturdy individualist in Europe. The danger there is not of collectivist socialism, but of anarchism or syndicalism. If Franco fails, it is not probable that the Marxists and the anarchists

386

will come to terms. Both are revolutionary, but the one party wishes the State to be everything the other wishes the State to be nothing. In Spain, alone among the countries of Europe, radical individualism is still powerful. As both are equally ruthless, and as the Nationalists seem to be not lambs either, the prospects for this unhappy country are black enough.

But they will win through somehow, for they are a singularly healthy race, and during the long period of their obscurity, when superficial observers spoke of their decadence, they were really recuperating after the exhausting centuries of war, glory and religious fanaticism.

There are anabolic and catabolic periods in history—periods when force is being stored, and periods when it is being squandered. The spendthrift nation has a short life and a merry one; then it has to keep quiet for one or more centuries.